Phyllis Kohl Coston

CELEBRATION
—— *of* ——
SUCCESS

PHYLLIS KOHL COSTON

authorHOUSE®

AuthorHouse™
1663 Liberty Drive
Bloomington, IN 47403
www.authorhouse.com
Phone: 1-800-839-8640

© 2013 Phyllis Kohl Coston. All rights reserved.

No part of this book may be reproduced, stored in a retrieval system, or transmitted by any means without the written permission of the author.

Published by AuthorHouse 8/5/2013

ISBN: 978-1-4918-0231-1 (sc)
ISBN: 978-1-4918-0233-5 (hc)
ISBN: 978-1-4918-0232-8 (e)

Library of Congress Control Number: 2013913229

Any people depicted in stock imagery provided by Thinkstock are models, and such images are being used for illustrative purposes only.
Certain stock imagery © Thinkstock.

This book is printed on acid-free paper.

Because of the dynamic nature of the Internet, any web addresses or links contained in this book may have changed since publication and may no longer be valid. The views expressed in this work are solely those of the author and do not necessarily reflect the views of the publisher, and the publisher hereby disclaims any responsibility for them.

DEDICATION

I am dedicating *Celebration of Success* to the millions of people who cope with learning disabilities.

I am also dedicating this book to three special people who supported and encouraged me as I wrote it:

Herb Coston, my husband and best friend. Herb was thoughtful in many, many ways. He supported me and did numerous tasks, giving me time to write *Celebration of Success*. It would take the entire page to write the list of all he did. I especially thank him for diligently proofreading and editing all of the chapters after they were skyped and edited. He is the "Best of the Best!"

Peggy Ferrell, my seminary roommate. Together we spent many hours skyping and editing every chapter. Peggy was able to find the right word or phrase when I couldn't express my idea. She was always encouraging me and giving me good advice. She is a wonderful friend!

Debbie Leigh, the Assistant to the Dean of the Chapel of West Virginia Wesleyan College. Often as I wrote, the computer would "fight me." When I called her for help, Debbie would discover my problem and relieve my frustration. She also read and reflected on some of the stories, sharing her ideas and opinions. I really appreciate her help and thoughtfulness.

TABLE OF CONTENTS

Preface ix
Acknowledgements xi
Introduction xiii

Adam Oberkircher.. 1
Tim O'Connell...7
Chuck Buck 11
Fred Langsam... 15
Evan Tracey.. 20
Allison Mohan Tracey 25
Laura Overly Fisher... 33
Isaac Willis 44
Fred Conklin 54
Andrew Collins 60
Tom Merrill's Guys: Jamie Fluke, Gregg McFarland, and Jim Chiang . 65
Diane Leo Menorca... 75
Paul Virant 82
Laura Rogers Ellis 85
Jonathan Langsam 89
Jennifer Shaw Fosko... 97
Amy Shearman O'Brien 103
Katherine Kimes 107
Mark Dangora.. 112

| vii

James Hoffman	121
Alice Babson	126
Amy	133
Matthew Wallace	137
Robert Hogan	142
Emily Patton Hogan	146
Christopher Kellogg	150
Catherine Eldridge	153
Patricia Boothe	158
Jack Ewing	163
John Edward Ciszek III	169
Bryan Baker	177
Kelly Pollard Paxton	187
Karim Badwan	192
Jennifer Buza	197
Jeffrey Kulinsky	201
Nick Selan	207
Tips for Parents	213
Tips for Teachers	219
In Memoriam	225

PREFACE

"You are stupid"; "My little sister in second grade reads better than you"; "You go to the Retard Class." These are the taunts heard by the people whose stories you will read. Some teachers and counselors added to the problem by remarks: "You will never go to college," "You need a vocation in which you can use your hands," "You can't handle a college prep course," "College for Y0U—You are kidding yourself," "No college will ever accept you."

These students were accepted by a quality institution, West Virginia Wesleyan College, to participate in a Special Service Program designed to give support to college students with Learning Disabilities. This program began before the Americans With Disabilities Act for college students was passed, making Wesleyan a pioneer.

Although the special program was not begun until 1982, the Learning Center had been helping students for almost 20 years, and was known in West Virginia and in other states, where I had been privileged to speak or help start study skills programs.

I met with Hal Latimer, the president of Wesleyan, to ask for his permission to start a special program. He was very willing to support this venture. He liked the idea because it was service oriented and fit the mission of the college, without creating a cost problem. With his support and the support of his successor, Thomas Courtice, the program grew, more staff members were added, and students applied from all over the country.

Today the current president, Dr. Pamela Balch, is also very supportive of Wesleyan's Learning Center. She has shared the following comments for the readers:

"The true life stories in the book will tug at your heart and will convince you that we must continue to support programs that build student confidence, leadership, academic success, organizational skills, and positive attitudes.

Personally, I want to thank the author, Dr. Phyllis Coston, for this book. Phyllis is like the little energizer bunny who never gave up on a student. Her students became entrepreneurs, public relations specialists, physicians, educators, counselors, political advisors, lawyers, artists, and business men and women.

Her messages will inspire educators to make a difference each and every day. Enjoy the stories that reaffirm our passion and commitment to enable students to reach their potential despite any and all obstacles."

ACKNOWLEDGEMENTS

I appreciate many friends and relatives who encouraged and helped me write *Celebration of Success*. I particularly want to share my appreciation and thanks to members of the West Virginia Wesleyan community. First, Dr. Pamela Balch, president, who has encouraged, helped and given good advice. Robert Skinner, Vice President for Advancement. Bob has answered questions and often pointed me in the right direction for help. Rochelle Long, Director of Public Relations, Marketing and Communication, who prepared the book for publication. The Members of the Alumni department, Kristi Wilkerson, Director of Alumni relations, who assisted in a variety of ways, and her staff members: Lynne Perry, Joanne DiStefano, and Leah Morehead who helped with research. The Computer Help Desk Staff, Supervisor Robert Burch, and Technical Specialists: Leon McKisic, Robert Osburn, Tom Reed, and Micah Snyder who solved many computer problems, and Angela Gay Kinkead, Dean of the chapel, who has given me support and encouragement.

Thanks to the parents of Learning disability children for all they do to help their sons and daughters succeed. I want to especially thank the women whom I interviewed for the chapter, "Tips for Parents": Judith Ciszic, Debbie Leigh, Lynn Neaves, Amy Shearman O'Brien, Becky Pollard, Claudette Rashid, Linda Selan, Theresa Wideman, and Buffy Wallace.

A special thanks to West Virginia Wesleyan's Learning Center Staff, past and present, whose dedication and love for students have helped them succeed.

INTRODUCTION

I founded West Virginia Wesleyan's Learning Center in 1963 and continued as director until my retirement in 1998. During those years the center was known as The Reading Center, The Reading and Study Skills Center, and finally The Learning Center. After retiring from The Learning Center, I again began teaching part time in the Christian Education Department, and I retired for the second time in 2009.

I am an ordained minister in the United Methodist Church and during my last year of teaching, I felt God tugging at my heart calling me to write this book, *Celebration of Success*. I felt motivated to encourage young people and others with learning disabilities to realize that they could succeed in whatever type of educational experience they needed to fulfill their dreams.

Another purpose of this book is to help persons with learning disabilities (LD) realize their learning disability may be "a gift" which should be considered a difference not a disability. The fact that a person's brain is wired differently has not only disadvantages (i.e. difficulty learning to read or focus,) but also advantages (i.e. visualizing things holistically or "outside the box"). I also want to help parents and teachers of LD students understand the importance of encouraging their children or students to recognize their successes and strengths and to help build their self-esteem. It is important to emphasize the necessity of counselors, students, and parents to work together in all areas of education. This includes helping students find colleges or technical schools offering programs that fit their student's needs, optimize their interests, and enhance their abilities to succeed.

Celebration of Success features short biographies of successful business and professional LD adults. There is a chapter with tips for parents and one with tips for teachers. There is also a chapter about a successful student with traumatic brain injuries. Each biography begins by introducing the person and concludes with that person's tips for success.

The adults in *Celebration of Success* were chosen randomly. During the fall of 2008 with the support of President Balch, Wesleyan's alumni office sent out surveys to the students who had been in the special program. Over a hundred surveys were returned; other recipients called or visited me. During the summer of 2009 a reunion, entitled "Celebration of Success" was held on campus. The alumni attending had their first interview for the book with me, my husband, or a learning center staff member. I interviewed them a second time by phone or personal visit. Others who are in the book called, visited Wesleyan, or I saw them while traveling and arranged an interview. There were a few I sought for a variety of reasons. All of them wanted to share their stories, hoping to help others. Only Amy wanted to include her story but preferred not to be identified.

Each person in the book reviewed a draft of his/her story to make corrections or changes. Their stories were rewritten to include these changes. Each was then edited, and proof read again. If any errors remain, the "buck" stops with me.

I have many more surveys with equally successful stories, but I feel it is time for me to bring closure to this project. I apologize to those who were willing to participate and are not included. I hope maybe their stories can be updated and shared some way in the future.

There are more biographies of men than women in the book, because there was a time when more boys than girls were diagnosed. I have a theory that this was because girls often cried when they were frustrated or failed. Boys often reacted aggressively, causing them to be sent to the principal's office. As a result of these behaviors boys were tested and girls were comforted but not tested. I hope today everyone who has a learning disability is diagnosed and receives the accommodations needed.

The students in this book began elementary school before the Americans with Disabilities Act was passed. For young people today many services are now required by The ADA. Although such requirements exist, some LD students avoid taking the risk of post-secondary education for fear of failure. Others avoid taking advantage of special programs for fear of being different. I hope the biographies in *Celebration of Success* reach these students and encourage them to be positive and to seek to understand themselves and especially the gifts God has given them. I also encourage young people to visit colleges, universities, technical, or vocational schools to learn about the accommodations and services each institution provides, and choose the school that "feels right" for meeting their special needs.

In closing, I want to thank all those who were willing to share their personal stories in *Celebration of Success.* For many it was painful to recall unpleasant memories. I join them in hoping that their experiences will help others on their life journeys.

Phyllis Kohl Coston

1995-96 West Virginia Wesleyan College Learning Center staff

ADAM OBERKIRCHER

Adam has had both disappointments and achievements in his journey to becoming a successful Physician Assistant. His first grade difficulty learning to read and write was typical of a dyslexic boy. Being goalie on a national champion soccer team in college was not typical. His life today is centered on his lovely wife Sandy, three children (Anna, Robert, and Alex), medicine, and staying healthy after a battle with cancer.

Adam's Story

Adam is dyslexic and because of it has worked very hard to be successful. He believes his biggest problem in school was dealing with his reading and spelling difficulties which lead to poor self-esteem. He was very frustrated in reading and spelling classes. Before being diagnosed with dyslexia, and due to his difficulty with spelling and reading, Adam was held back in 3rd grade and had to attend summer school yearly through all six of his elementary school years.

In 6th grade he was tested and diagnosed with dyslexia. He enrolled at The Gow School for dyslexic boys near Buffalo, NY. This was his best school experience. All the boys had similar problems to his, and the teachers knew how to deal with them. It was a great atmosphere for learning because of the small class sizes. While at Gow, Adam excelled in sports and eventually became co-captain of the varsity soccer team. While applying to colleges, Adam was offered a scholarship in soccer and lacrosse at New England College. He decided to turn it down so he could participate in the Learning Center Program at West Virginia Wesleyan.

He feels that Wesleyan was the right place for him to pursue education. He already knew that college would be difficult for him because he was informed upon graduation from Gow that he had a fourth grade spelling level and an eighth grade reading level. Adam felt that the extra learning tools offered at Wesleyan's Learning Center combined with hard work would help him accomplish his goals.

He said he particularly appreciated the way he was taught at the learning center. For instance Carolyn Mallory taught writing in the program with a kind and caring manner that helped Adam and others improve their confidence and self-esteem. Adam's grade point average (GPA) the first semester was not to be admired. However, as he adjusted to college life and improved his organizational skills, his grades improved. One aspect of college life that helped Adam was the camaraderie on the soccer team. Being a member of the 1994 and 1995 National Championship Soccer Teams and later being inducted as a team member into Wesleyan's Hall of Fame were two very positive experiences which helped Adam further develop the confidence to achieve his goals.

I remember a frustrating experience for Adam. He came into my office very dejected. I saw tears in his eyes. He was concerned about his science grades. He was making A's and B's in his other subjects, but in science he had C's. He knew he needed good grades in science to achieve his dream of being accepted into medical school. Adam's Grandfather, father, and uncles were all physicians. He wanted to care for people like they did. When I pointed out his high grades in Sociology and suggested a career in social work, he became upset and said, "You don't understand." He immediately got up and left the room. A few minutes later he returned and apologized for leaving so abruptly. When I asked him to explain, he told me that probably his children would have dyslexia and a social worker's salary would not be high enough to send them to the Gow School. This was true as Gow's tuition was higher than many colleges including Wesleyan's. We then looked at other areas of study. He decided to try business courses. Adam changed his major to business management and his minor to economics. He did well in both fields. He continued to be a well-rounded student, graduated in four years, and was president of the senior class.

After graduation, he was offered an accounting job in a Washington, DC law firm. Adam tells me that he still had the desire to go into medicine. What he had to overcome during this time was his own lack of belief in himself combined with ignoring the people in his life who believed that a career in medicine was out of his reach. He decided to study more sciences and to prove to himself that he could put his knowledge to work. While working and supporting himself, he took science classes at night from the University of Maryland. He also had a wonderful opportunity to volunteer at Zacchaeus' Free Medical Clinic which served the homeless and uninsured of Washington D.C. They had a medical training program to teach their volunteers how to draw blood, perform tests using microscopy and bacteriology, and how to properly interview and triage patients. When Adam initially visited the clinic and applied to their medical training program, they told him there were no openings. However, they were interested in him for his accounting and bookkeeping skills. Adam told them he would think about volunteering. He felt frustrated as he left the clinic because of not getting into the training program. As he walked down the street through the homeless and prostitute areas, he began to believe that God was testing him. "It was at that moment that I saw my selfishness and made the decision to volunteer at the clinic in whatever capacity they needed." The staff at the free medical clinic was elated when he volunteered to help them. Coincidently, three weeks after starting, a person dropped out of the medical training program and the position was offered to Adam. His success at the free medical clinic was complemented by honors in his science classes.

After continuing his work in the law office and volunteering four years at the free medical clinic, he decided to return to Buffalo, NY. His grandmother had died and he felt his grandfather needed him. He looked for a way to continue his pursuit of medicine, and took a volunteer position in a research lab at Roswell Park Cancer Institute

(RPCI) in Buffalo. Here he started at the lowest level, but eventually began to learn important laboratory skills such as DNA isolation and other analysis techniques. These were difficult times because he wasn't paid, so he would donate bone marrow to earn $200 every six weeks to pay for a cheap apartment and food. He was accepted into the Masters of Science program at RPCI/ State University of New York at Buffalo. Through the Master's program, he was able to take medical school classes such as histology, biochemistry, and immunology. Through research he developed an early detection system to determine bone marrow transplant failure. While in the research lab, a strong work ethic was necessary, and the average work week was around 80 hours with some projects keeping him there over 24 hours. For his work, he became the first Master's student to publish a first authorship publication and went on to earn his name on multiple additional publications before earning his MS degree.

Through this journey, Adam learned that he had a passion for medicine and a desire to help people. This is when he applied to Medical school and was placed on the wait-list. A funny story that occurred around this time was how Adam heard about a group of Catholic nuns from the convent in Buffalo, who as part of their special ministry, prayed for people. He went to them and asked them to pray for him to be accepted into medical school. To show his appreciation, he caught fresh fish each week and brought his catch to them. Adam was also considering Physician Assistant School. It was at this time Adam decided that becoming a physician assistant would allow him to practice medicine and complete schooling in a more reasonable time. One reason for this was that his wife was expecting their first child, and he was eager to have time to be a good father. If he went the medical route, he would have four more years of medical school plus three to four years of residency. He also understood that because of his dyslexia, he would have to spend more time studying then others. He felt excited about his decision. In fact, he called me giving me the privilege to share his joy. In the end, Adam went back to the nuns asking them to stop praying for his acceptance into medical school. A week or so after talking to the nuns, he received his rejection letter from the medical school.

He then applied to Physician Assistant (PA) School and was accepted. PA school was not easy. He worked the hardest he ever had, taking classes from 8:00 AM to as late as 8:00 PM and then having to study all night. One class that was difficult for Adam was medical terminology. Adam said, "It wasn't the language of medicine that made it difficult, but rather having to spell everything correctly while taking timed examinations. I remember the stress of taking 28 credit hours in one semester and having 15 final exams in seven days when I only had time to study for 5 exams. I remember passing my breaking point and looking figuratively back at the line and feeling like I was in no-mans-land. After passing the exams, I felt like I literally shook for two weeks." Going through this with an infant and a toddler was tough, but he received great support from his wife Sandy. Adam also found comfort in discussing the stresses of school with his father. His father was encouraging and supportive while sharing his own stories of difficulties while in medical school.

He worked very hard, enjoyed his classes, and earned good grades. During his rotation period he had several experiences that he still remembers. During his first week of rotation, Adam diagnosed a woman with ruptured diverticulitis and saved her life by setting up an emergency surgery. He also enjoyed rotating through Surgery and Emergency Room duty. All of the practical experiences during this time were important to him. However, his happiness was short lived. In his senior year he encountered two of the worst experiences of his life. One was losing his father to a painful cancer, and the second one was because he was dyslexic. The Dean of the PA school called Adam in to see him. The dean then proceeded to tell Adam that he didn't believe that an LD student had the right to go into medicine, and he would try to prevent his graduation. Adam was angry. His grades were good and he had worked hard to be successful. **This was not fair!**

He went immediately to the dean of students. He was still angry when he told her his story and angrily stated he would sue the school. This dean was a kind woman. She listened to Adam and recognized his frustration. She told him she would handle the situation and he should not worry. **He would graduate!** Adam will always remember her.

Following graduation, Adam passed his national boards and began working in cardiothoracic surgery. After one year, he changed jobs and took a position at Roswell Park Cancer Institute as a physician assistant in Radiation Medicine where he continues to work today. He chose to work with Oncology patients because of his previous research, the loss of his father and sister to cancer, and his own battle with cancer. He felt that with all the adversity he had fought through, he would be a positive voice to his patients during their difficult times in treatment.

Adam knows he made the right decision to become a physician assistant and has since passed his national re-certification examinations twice. He loves his wife and family and has time to be with them. He is also very happy that none of their children are dyslexic and that his early fears were unfounded. As many others have, Adam believes he has turned his experience with dyslexia into a gift that he uses daily to help others. Following treatment of his own cancer, Adam decided to fight his way back to good health and celebrates that through participating in triathlons such as the Iron Man competitions. Adam agreed to share his story in the hope that it would encourage other learning disabled students to find their inner strengths and accomplish their goals.

Adam shared the following tips:

1. Remember life is short; it's a gift, and a wonderful journey.
2. Your hardest times, the times forged from grit and determination, will be your biggest character building moments.

1986 Soccer Team

TIM O'CONNELL

Tim is a 1988 graduate of West Virginia Wesleyan College, married to Sheryl Watts, a 1990 graduate of Wesleyan where they met as students. They are the parents of two teenagers, Jack and Devon. They are a great family. At present Tim's career is in Medical Technology in Coventry, Connecticut.

Tim's Story

Tim is dyslexic and has struggled with the problems that many dyslexics face, but his positive attitude and coping skills he has learned have allowed him to succeed. His problems began in elementary school. He recalls a painful experience in second grade. It was in spelling class. The teacher dictated the words. After writing them, the students corrected their own tests by looking at the correct spelling on the board. Tim, an achiever, was pleased as he had a 100%. His happiness was short lived when the teacher went around checking the work. She said he did not make 100%. He had misspelled ***probably***. He protested that it was correct as it was exactly the same as the word on the board. He was embarrassed when the teacher showed him the correct spelling and what he had done wrong. He was upset because he thought the other students were laughing at him. Tim is the youngest of 6 children; all were good students. He was motivated to succeed.

He knew his family expected him to do well and he didn't want to disappoint them.

In fourth grade when there was more emphasis on reading subject material such as science and social studies, and more required writing, he began to struggle more. He felt he had more trouble than other kids comprehending material. When he read, the words kept jumping all over the page, and he couldn't follow them. His family, realizing his frustration, was concerned. They discussed his problem with members of the Orton Society, an organization dedicated to the study of dyslexia. They were able to help by having Tim tested. Dyslexia was confirmed.

Even though Tim's dyslexia was diagnosed, most teachers in the 1970's and 1980's had not been trained to understand learning disabilities. Many did not even believe dyslexia really existed. The Americans With Disabilities Act was not passed until 1990, and Tim, like many others, needed accommodations that were not available in most schools.

Tim's parents felt that since the public school was not helping him, it would be good for Tim to go to a boarding school like his brothers and sisters did when they were in eighth grade. They enrolled him in a boarding school in Maine. Academically it was a good school and he enjoyed it, but they did not have teachers trained to teach dyslexics.

When Tim was in high school, his parents knew he was struggling but was motivated to succeed. As a result they began looking for other schools. They discovered Gow, a school for dyslexic boys near Buffalo, New York. Tim and one other boy were the first seniors that Gow School accepted. It was just the right place for him and at last he experienced academic success!

The faculty at Gow understood the problems of dyslexics and had developed methods to help them achieve success. Tim remembers Mark Kimble, the headmaster, who helped him write his 40 page paper on horses. To write a paper of that length, he had lots of material, but had problems organizing the information. Mr. Kimble taught him to outline. Outlining was a wonderful skill to learn and he uses it today in his work when writing technical manuals and teaching others to use them.

Tim said he will always be grateful for the study techniques he learned at Gow and Wesleyan. Tim particularly remembers using the book, *Using Both Sides of the Brain,* by Tony Buzzan, in Wesleyan's Study Skills Class. There he discovered that he was right hemisphered and he began using the techniques that went with his style of learning. This understanding has been helpful both in college and in his career.

Tim found his reading comprehension really improved when he learned to "chunk" words, which is seeing a group of words all at once. Since the brain's short term memory can only hold seven items at a time, Tim would lose the beginning of sentences when he tried to read a long sentence word by word; by "chunking" he was able to understand what he was reading. This is a method that has stayed with him when he reads. It is a method useful for everyone.

Tim was at Wesleyan when the Learning Center had the first Computer Lab on campus. He said the computer was "the best thing since sliced bread". It was helpful in college and is important in his work today. The spell checker and proof readers made all the difference between writing good papers or fair papers. He realized even with the spell checker, he needed a proof reader. He still uses proof readers for his writing today. This is something all writers should do because the spell checkers do not correct everything. Tim not only uses proofreaders, but amazingly for a dyslexic, has also become a proofreader himself!

After graduating from Wesleyan, Tim began a career in retailing and was very successful. He received promotions and was in management several times including *Service Merchandise*, a regional retail chain store.

After a successful career in retailing, Tim began working for a consulting firm, *Strategic Applications International Corporation*. (SAIC). Here he focused on Computer software for hospitals. Today, his current title is *Epic Senior Business Analyst*. Among his many duties he develops training manuals and teaches others how to use the manual and the software. He is known as an understanding, caring teacher for his work with the adults who are learning how to use the application software and follow the manual. The first day of class he shares with them about his dyslexia, and he assures them that he understands some will struggle with this class. He tells them, "I will make sure everyone will graduate and do well." He helps them reach this goal. He often works at night with an individual to help him/her achieve success. The "gift of dyslexia" enables him to help others.

Tim also likes to share with others various ways to cope with their dyslexia or other learning disabilities. In his professional career, Tim has been required to take several certification exams. He recommends to any adult with a learning disability to use any and all resources at their disposal. Most professional organizations will offer extended time to individuals who have to take tests. The 1990 ADA law is not limited to those in school. He has found that extended time is important when taking the certification tests.

Tim and Sheryl have been married for 23 years and have two wonderful teen age children, Jack and Devon, who work hard in school and are honor students. Jack has inherited Dyslexia and has to work extra hard to achieve. Tim and Sheryl have worked with the school in seeing that Jack gets all the accommodations he needs. Tim's experience and knowledge of the ADA law have been helpful. Jack appreciates the computer, but also the Kindle Fire, a useful tool for reading. He finds changing the white screen background to a black screen with white letters improves his reading.

Tim and Sheryl support their children and are proud of them. Tim offered to take them anywhere in the world if they made straight A's for a year. Devon reached that goal and he and Devon are going to China. Tim realizes that this is a very difficult goal for Jack because of his dyslexia. He rewarded him for being an honor student by a family trip to Hawaii, the place Jack wanted to go. Tim wants to instill the belief in his children that if you work hard and learn as much as you can, the world is yours to capture.

Although Tim is busy with work and family, he takes time about twice a month for his hobby, flying. In 2003 he earned a pilot's license. This is a difficult task for a dyslexic. Many told him he could not become a pilot, but he was motivated. Once again he has succeeded and enjoys flying.

TIM'S TIPS FOR SUCCESS:

1. Never give up, especially don't give up on yourself.
2. Look at the positive in situations.
3. When faced with challenges, believe there is always another option.
4. Never stop learning.

CHUCK BUCK

Chuck Buck is a successful salesman for a real estate agency in Charleston, South Carolina. He is happily married and has two children. He has worked hard to succeed and his story should be helpful to others. When people meet Chuck they realize he is a successful man. However, this success did not come easily. He worked to cope with his dyslexia and to do his best in his careers.

Chuck Buck's Story

Chuck is an outstanding salesman who has had several jobs in sales since graduating from Wesleyan in 1989. Presently, he is the Broker-in-Charge of residential sales for Carnes Crossroads, a 2500 acre mixed use real estate development. At its time of completion this project will be its own town with 15,000 residents and over 3500 homes. It will also include a retail-commercial component. This is a long range project and Chuck is dedicated to seeing it through to completion.

Chuck's wife, Jesse, is a first grade teacher. They have two teen age children, Trey and Lee, both of whom are active in sports and are avid lacross players. Since Trey is searching for the best college for him, they have hired a college coach for him. This individual tries to match the right student with the right school.

All through school, Chuck had a reading problem which frustrated and embarrassed him. He still read on the 3rd grade level when he was in 12th grade. He feared being called on to read aloud. One way he coped with the problem was to go to the bathroom when it was his turn to read. Being a behavior problem was another method of coping. Despite these problems, Chuck credits a lot of his career success to his learning disability. He feels it allowed, or even forced him to sharpen his social skills and made him a much better salesman and manager. Also, since he had to work harder than others to do well in school, the additional hard work gave him a very strong work ethic which is still helpful in his career.

Success in reading was so seldom for Chuck that he vividly remembers a successful reading experience when he was in junior high. A Sunday school teacher called on him to read the 23rd Psalm. It was too late for him to leave the room, but he read it with no mistakes. He was so pleased and excited that he read it 10 times to his mother when he got home. This experience helped him overcome his fear of reading out loud in front of his peers and built his self confidence, of which he had little or none at the time.

Chuck's problem in reading may have been not only caused by his dyslexia, but might also have been impacted by his frequent moves due to his father's work. During his school years he attended schools in Houston, Texas, Greenville, S C., back to Houston, Texas, and then to Lancaster PA. Chuck learned how to make friends because it was vital to his surviving in new settings. This skill helped him learn how to be accepted then, and continues to be important in his career.

Sports in junior high school and high school helped him cope with his problems and be accepted in school. It also allowed him to meet a new group of friends. After graduating from high school, his family took him to a career/ guidance counselor to help him in choosing the right college. He made a commitment to his parents that he would go to college for only one semester and then they would make a decision about his continuing in college. His parents knew that they had one shot to make graduating from college happen and they did everything and anything possible to make this a good experience for him. The counselor recommended Landmark Preparatory School which was well known for working with dyslexics and having a low teacher student ratio. Landmark's admission director told Chuck's parents that attending Landmark would be tax deductable, which was helpful when it came to the financial burden of such an expensive school. Following this advice, Chuck attended summer school and a post graduate year at Landmark and graduated reading on 12th grade level. He then looked at several colleges with special support programs and chose West Virginia Wesleyan.

Chuck took seriously his opportunity to be in college. "I always remember I could hear the speakers of my fraternity house blasting music while I had to sit in the library and study; not an easy choice for me to make, but I knew I only had one chance to make my college career happen. My parents didn't have the financial ability to send me to multiple colleges. It was a one and only opportunity for me and I had to give it my best."

Chuck is an optimist and sees his glass as half full and not as half empty. He has used his outgoing personality to help compensate for his disability. It allows him to use his skills advantageously in his work (although there are times of frustration with today's environment which includes formal letters, e-mails, texting, etc.) Sometimes Chuck can't get words spelled closely enough for a spell checker to even recognize them. "It is critical to my success to have the right administrator in place who knows my weaknesses and my strengths so we can work together as a team. I am much better with people face to face than I am in front of a key board, which I find challenging." Many have heard of the 80/20 rule, in which 20% of the people do 80% of the business. Chuck has set the bar higher. He likes a 90/10 rule, which means he seeks to hire those who are 10%ers to work with him so that together they can accomplish 90% of the work. He believes that is a big secret to success.

Chuck appreciates his parents who were very supportive both finically and emotionally as he pursued his academic career. Today his wife and children are also supportive. The family enjoys each other and is proud of each individual's successes.

Chuck shares the following tips:

1. Don't give up.
2. Find someone with whom to share your frustrations.
3. Try twice as hard as anyone else.
4. Studies first and socialize second.
5. A small class setting is helpful.
6. Don't be too embarrassed or "cool" to get additional support (tutors always help and they are sometimes good looking).

Chuck Buck with tutor

FRED LANGSAM

I magine yourself as a third grader. You are in a reading class. There are four groups. Three groups have nine or ten children in each and are reading primary grade books. The fourth is your group and you are the only person in it. Your book is a kindergarten book. Your friends call it a baby book. How do you feel? This third grader with the "baby book" was Fred Langsam, a 1989 West Virginia Wesleyan College graduate and a special education support teacher today!

Fred's Story

When Fred was in the early primary grades, he couldn't read or write. He shed many tears and kept asking himself, "What's wrong with me?" He was very frustrated and was really relieved when the school suggested to his parents that he be tested for a learning disability. He is sure now that there were many clues before third grade, but schools and teachers were not attuned to them in the 1970's.

After the testing, it was a relief to be bussed to another school and become part of a self-contained class room. Bussing continued in the 4th and 5th grades. Here he had an outstanding young teacher. Under her guidance he learned phonics which opened the door to reading for him. The atmosphere in her class room was great and he felt free to talk a lot in class which helped improve his self-image. He knows now that he is an auditory and visual learner and she provided opportunities for him to learn using these strengths.

Middle school was another frustrating experience. Fred was so embarrassed by his inability to write. Technology and use of the computer were not part of the school scene then. His mother who worked with emotionally disturbed kids understood the frustrations students experience in school. She was very helpful by writing for him as he dictated. He remembers those days and appreciates her today.

High school was better. Fred still hated academics but he loved sports and played football, wrestled, and managed a team. He also enjoyed working after school in a restaurant where he did dishes and learned to cook. He felt he used his auditory and tactile skills which made him effective. (He believes that the best chefs are learning disabled.) When he was a high school senior he was in the work study program which allowed him to spend part of his day working at a pizza place. He not only worked there but also became the manager. He probably would have had a career in restaurant management, but his parents and others expected him to attend college.

Teachers can always make a difference and an English teacher made the difference for him. Fred was in high school but had never read a book. The teacher encouraged him to read *Catcher in the Rye*. He read it out loud to himself and loved it! This book captured his imagination. He had never been able to picture characters in his head, but reading this book out loud allowed him to visualize them.

Fred had another great experience that turned him on to learning. Between high school and college he lived on a Kibbutz in Israel for three months and did a dig outside of Tel Aviv. He was able to build on his strengths using his verbal skills to share and understand the culture. This experience whet his appetite for learning and helped make him ready for college.

Because of Fred's severe learning disability it was important for him to attend a college that had a support program, small classes, and professors who were willing to see students individually, allowing them to listen and talk with each other. Wesleyan fit those criteria. He had good experiences and professors, but several stand out as being particularly helpful. Dr. Morrissette was one. Even though he had large classes, there was time for discussion. Opportunities to meet in his office and share essays with him verbally instead of writing them allowed Fred to show his knowledge without the embarrassment of writing. Computers were new in the educational world at that time, and became available to Fred at Wesleyan. Fred still didn't have the ability to write in complex sentences, but he was a "great talker." The encouragement he received by sharing short essays verbally allowed him to feel confident in using the computer to write longer research papers. As a result he majored in government.

Art and speech communication classes also allowed Fred to use his strengths and he minored in these two areas. Art classes had a real impact on him. Professor Van Nostrum had a way of helping him reach a different part of his brain. Professor Van Nostrum ran his world in an unusual way. It was powerful for Fred who learned to use his hands in a different way than writing. As a result he produced special creative art work. He not only learned more about his brain, but also found it was a calming experience.

Fred especially appreciated the caring staff of the learning center, and the study skills class. He was helped, for instance, by learning the method of mapping to take notes. Mapping allowed him to write words or short sentences to get the main ideas. This system met his learning style. Today, Fred shares this method with students who learn in ways similar to him.

When Fred finished college, he thought about following in his father's footsteps and becoming a lawyer. However, even though he passed the law school entrance exam, he changed his mind. He had taken a job as a teacher's assistant and loved working with the children. He went back to school and got a Master's Degree in Teaching and later an administration certificate. After graduation, he taught two years in Louisville, Kentucky before returning to Montgomery County to begin teaching there.

Fred has been teaching special education in Montgomery County for over twenty years. He was also a student support specialist for a year and an assistant principal for two years. Currently he is a behavior support teacher. He works with emotionally impaired students and their teachers. This includes helping find appropriate strategies that will work for students who have learning and behavioral issues. Fred wants to help teachers understand what is going on with some of these children, and to make learning less painful. He reminds teachers that for some students with learning disabilities, reading is ten times harder because of their difficulty in processing. Reading out loud is extremely difficult for many. Fred believes you have to be taught to read out loud and practice being fluent. He hated reading groups in which students took turns to read aloud individually. He would try to figure out when his turn would come and practice, practice, practice in his head. Then he could read like others. Fred's personal experiences are helpful for him today.

Fred believes it is so important to find the right teacher for the right child. He feels gifted because he is able to match students with teachers. One of Fred's philosophies is that being in the right classroom with the right teacher is vital for success. A student can recover from two bad placements, but not three. He knows some teachers are good with one type of student, but can't reach another. Having the right teachers was the key to his college success, and he wants this for all students at every grade level. (As a professor I believe that this is because we teach the way we learn and we are more understanding and effective with students who share our learning style.)

Fred works with students who have not been able to succeed in their school placement. They not only have a learning disability but emotional problems as well. Much of his work is one on one and very intense. He realizes that allowing the student to enjoy the teacher's company can become a powerful experience. Knowing the teacher believes in him and cares about him brings hope and a feeling of success.

Fred knows technology has been helpful for him and others with learning disabilities. He learned to read, but writing by hand has always been a problem. Although he is good in his job and communicates effectively orally, he has never felt comfortable writing. However, society has changed, making him feel more comfortable. Computers helped. Now he can text and twitter and not be looked down on because short sentences are okay. He has a different attitude because he isn't embarrassed but accepted.

A learning disability never goes away, but you can learn coping strategies. Fred advises young people today to:

1. Find what works for you.
2. Believe you can do anything.
3. If reading processing and fluency are difficult accept that, but ask for help and practice.
4. Use technology.
5. Be self-confident and accept yourself.

EVAN TRACEY

Evan Tracey is a 1989 West Virginia Wesleyan Graduate who is now senior vice president of communications for the American Coalition for Clean Coal Electricity. He is married to Allison Mohan, a West Virginia Wesleyan 1992 graduate. They are the parents of 3 sons. In his story Evan shares his belief that his dyslexia is a gift and he challenges those with LD to succeed by looking positively at their learning difference.

Evan Tracey's Story

Evan's learning disability was discovered by an elderly nun at Little Flower Catholic School in Bethesda, MD. His parents followed her recommendation and had him tested. The diagnosis of dyslexia was confirmed. Following the diagnosis his family sent him to the Kingsbury Center in Washington, DC, for help.

Evan was a typical dyslexic: smart, but having difficulties in reading, spelling, etc. and feeling frustrated, not knowing what was wrong. As a result of his frustration he rebelled and became a trouble maker. The school was not equipped to handle LD students. Largely for behavior issues he was asked to leave Little Flower Catholic School. He transferred to the public school for the 7th grade.

Although it was a good public school system, they also were not prepared to work with students who had learning disabilities, as schools are today. Trouble makers, discipline problems, and students with learning disabilities were all put into classes together. This was a bad situation for a smart student like Evan. Finally Evan realized he didn't belong in these classes. They were too easy and he knew the longer he stayed the more likely it would be that he might become part of the wrong crowd and not succeed in anything.

He knew he needed more difficult classes to stay connected with his friends. Evan's father and mother agreed with him that he ought to go into the challenging classes, but told him to realize that he would have to "sink or swim." His father was the type of person who made it clear that his faith in him meant Evan had to take on this responsibility and not fall behind. Evan went to the school counselor and principal and said, "I don't belong in those classes, and I want the opportunity to sink or swim." The principal and guidance counselor both listened and accepted his request. The classes were more difficult. He still had a tough time reading and had a poor attention span, but he worked hard, accepting his father's challenges and made C's and B's in difficult classes. Evan says that there were some teachers along the way to whom he owes great credit because they would not allow him to be lazy or give in to the hard work. Several gave him special help and after school tutoring. His 7th grade math teacher was always willing to give him extra help, giving up personal time to tutor him and making Evan realize he was not to fail but to use dyslexia as a reason to succeed.

His father's attitude of working hard carried through in all areas of life. When Evan was a teenager, he wanted something that was rather expensive. His father told him he would think about it and give him his decision the next afternoon. He met Evan that afternoon and gave him a lawnmower. He told Evan if you want something, you earn the money to pay for it. Evan was always very hard working and open to the challenges his father gave him in regard to both work and school. This helped Evan develop his work ethic in all phases of life. His father's advice has played a big part in Evan's success today.

Evan did not "sink," but met the challenges of the difficult classes. He had to work harder than most other students because of reading slowly and having a poor attention span. It was clear to Evan and his father that the more he had on his plate the better he did in school. For Evan, too much time was a bad thing. He felt he had truly accomplished his goal when he received his high school diploma.

The next step was college. His high school counselor and his parents helped him make the decision to attend West Virginia Wesleyan because of the reputation of the Special Support Program. As soon as he participated in the orientation weekend, he realized this was the right choice. He had worried it might be like high school, but it wasn't. The students in the Special Support Program were like him. They wanted to be challenged and accepted as regular freshmen, not LD students. It had been hard in high school to find kids that Evan felt were like him. Coming to college was a genuine awakening because the classmates who became his friends offered a real peer experience making him feel he was not alone with his struggles.

Evan realized you can't fake it in college, and that is one reason he was the type of student any study skills teacher loves to have in class. He not only listened to learn about recommended skills, but he used them. He says he still uses them today. He felt like he finally knew how to learn material and engage in new passions like writing and public speaking, two things he had feared before going to college. He really did conquer this fear as he has been a featured speaker at many forums and conferences.

Evan commented that the Learning Center was great, and he especially appreciated what he learned about the brain. He said he realized the way you are wired makes a difference in studying, listening in class, and in every area of life. Because of this insight, he became confident his freshman year that he could use his LD to succeed, not fail.

Evan was not only helped by the Learning Center, but had other good opportunities. He really appreciated many of his classes and professors. His fraternity helped him develop leadership skills. A speech he had to give when he really wasn't prepared made him realize he could speak extemporaneously very well. These experiences helped him to continue to develop a good self-concept.

A very difficult event occurred between his junior and senior year; his father died. Evan's father had been a great source of encouragement and support all his life. With the death of his father, Evan knew he couldn't take five years to graduate, as many of his friends were doing, so he worked hard to finish in four years. At that time the only help he received from the Learning Center was recorded text books and untimed tests. The study tips he learned his freshman year, such as the importance of preparation and knowing how to use time wisely, were important to his academic success.

Evan continued his education after graduating from Wesleyan. He received an MA from George Mason University International Institute in Arlington, Va.

In 1996 Evan founded Kantar Media's Campaign Media Analysis Group (CMAG), which became the nation's top strategic media research company for politics and public affairs advertising. As CMAG President, Evan was on-air media consultant to CNN, spoke on political and advocacy media at over 75 schools and forums, wrote numerous commentaries for various advertising bureaus and groups, and wrote a regular column for *Ad Age Magazine.* He has been a member of the faculty at George Washington University Graduate School of Political Management since 2006, teaching on communications and communication strategy.

In his present position as Senior Vice President of Communications for the American Coalition for Clean Coal Electricity, Evan's duties include setting direction and strategy for a $40 million campaign to help form public opinion and public policy relevant to the coal based electricity industry. The list of media he uses is very comprehensive.

Evan met his wife, Allison Mohan, at Wesleyan. She was in the Special Support Program and is a Wesleyan graduate whose story also appears in this book. She was a teacher for ten years and is a wonderful wife and mother to their 3 children.

A young person with a learning disability today can be especially helped by Evan's philosophy and advice. He believes his dyslexic brain is a gift because he is creative and can "think out of the box." He said he wouldn't trade his ability to problem solve in order to become a better reader or speller. He feels dyslexia has helped him in his public speaking as he can put things the way people can understand. This has been especially true in the graduate classes he has taught. His dyslexia made him realize he had to work hard and believe in himself. This latter advice is good for all LD students; in fact it is good for everyone. Evan's advice is to believe in yourself and work until you find out how to succeed; never just expect to fail or give up.

ALLISON MOHAN TRACEY

Allison Tracey is a wonderful woman, wife, and mother. She is dedicated to her family. As a stay at home mom, she encourages her children to accept their gifts. She challenges them to never give up, and tries to help them develop a positive self-esteem. She is a 1992 West Virginia Wesleyan graduate, married to Evan Tracey whose story is also in this book.

Allison's Story

Allison enjoyed her professional career of teaching for ten years. She continued teaching after her first son, Cameron, was born. When he was two years old, her second son, Luke, joined the family. She enjoyed her boys and realized she didn't want to miss opportunities to be with her preschool sons, so she decided to become a full time wife and mother. Her third son, Will, was born two years later. She knows being with her family was the right decision.

One of the skills Allison needed to develop as a student at Wesleyan was utilizing organizational skills, which she accomplished. When she was single, she was able to go to graduate school and work three jobs. Now with a busy husband and three boys she appreciates the ability to organize, and recognizes it as a life skill she constantly uses. Allison faces challenges with her sons' ever changing school and numerous sports schedules as well as her personal schedule. Although she doesn't recommend more than one sport at a time, she feels when children are young they need to explore their interests.

Since the Tracey's large calendar is full, Allison has been teaching her two older sons the necessity of planning ahead and keeping a schedule. She is a very visual person and finds color coding a helpful tool for her. She helps the boys utilize this skill by color coding different events, sports, and activities on the calendar. All this helps in organizing and planning as a family. She recognizes that she and Evan need personal space and time also. Allison talks to the boys about the necessity of a calendar so they understand that you can't just go to someone's house or have them over for supper without planning ahead. She has also emphasized they must check the calendar to understand the needs of others in the family. For instance, Cameron plays the trumpet; is in the school band; and participates in the alter service at church. He puts his events on the calendar and reviews the daily activities before school. This helps him take ownership of his life. She and Evan believe this kind of planning teaches responsibility and consideration for others as well as helping the boys learn life skills such as time management, the importance of being a team member, and ownership of calendar details.

Allison is pleased that the school is now emphasizing organizational skills and she tries to reinforce this at home. In the evening before going to bed, she has her boys put their assignments in their back packs and have their binders ready. Clothes and shoes are also in place so that mornings are not stressful. She was pleased when Cameron came home from school and told her that putting his work in order was a great idea. He felt sorry for a friend who got in trouble because he couldn't find his work. This was an "ah ha moment" for him. It was good for her to hear that a connection he made at school was based on the ideals they have at home. Allison believes we learn from both our own mistakes and the mistakes of others. She not only encourages the boys to be prepared for daily assignments, but also for long range projects. She recommends beginning immediately and setting a completion date two weeks earlier than work is due.

One of the advantages of being a "stay at home mom" is that she has been able to volunteer at the school and see how her children participate in class. This enables her to be better prepared for working with them on their homework. As a result, she was able to recognize that Cameron might have a learning disability. She and Evan prefer using the term "learning differences" (which we used at Wesleyan's Learning Center) to the term "learning disabilities." Since she and Evan both have learning differences, they asked that Cameron be tested before he had serious problems in school. This was done and their diagnosis was confirmed. They received a learning profile for Cameron. Allison is always appreciative of teachers who listen to her. These teachers realize that they may only see Cameron an hour a day, but Allison is with him a greater amount of time. The teachers also know that Allison listens to them. They have genuine respect for each other and a good relationship.

Both Allison and Evan believe a learning disability (difference) can be a gift. Accepting the concept of a learning difference as a gift is important. Instead of saying, "Poor me," you can try to determine your strengths and meet your challenges by working hard to accomplish a task. This is what Allison and Evan have done in their lives. They are both successful today. As a result, they are motivating their children to work hard also. When their children have problems with homework or a special project, they remind them to say, "I know I can do this! Nothing will stop me!" They have taught them to remember these three challenges: work hard, double check your work, and never turn in your first draft. Although this is Evan's and Allison's philosophy, it is not easy for their boys to accept when they would rather be outside playing. Allison understands this, but tells them, "You don't get credit for just doing work, only for doing **good** work. Everything you do represents **you**." She has tried to encourage them to be like their dad, to be an expert in their project by exploring and finding a great deal of information. They then know they can stand proudly behind their work.

Allison is pleased that they are developing a family culture of cooperation among the boys. If mom is busy, an older brother can help a younger one with homework. For instance, when Luke had a big Spanish test his brother made flash cards for him, created a memory game, and then reviewed with him. Luke made a 100% on the test.

Both boys were proud. Their family likes to learn together by watching informational TV, traveling, and discussing these experiences. For them, learning is fun!

In addition to setting standards for work, Allison strives to help their children develop good self-concepts. Self-esteem is a high priority. You have to feel good about yourself to be motivated to achieve. She believes in praise for good work and accomplishments. She feels Evan is a good role model for the boys as they see him working hard and going over speeches several times to be ready to present them. Despite Evan's busy schedule he plays ball with them as soon as he comes home from work and he helps them with school work. He has shown them that "Hard work pays off in whatever you do." Allison has learned not to rush to do dishes after supper, but that spending time with the family and playing together is more important. Her children appreciate having family fun together. Since her children participate in sports, going as a family to games is very important.

Summer time offers many opportunities. However, as a teacher and a person with a learning difference, Allison knows that you can forget information over the summer. She keeps her children learning by doing art work, crafts, fun things on the iPad, and other interesting activities. August is the time for getting serious about going back to school and being prepared to do well by having organized time each day, usually about 15 or 20 minutes in the morning. She finds it important to keep a schedule and routine so that they can continue learning throughout the summer.

It has been advantageous for Allison to volunteer in her children's classrooms, to help them and the teachers. She is glad that she has an education background because she is able to ask the right questions, and can ask in a non-threatening way. The questions are helpful for clarification and to be aware of the accommodations Cameron is receiving. She and Evan want to know that he is receiving needed accommodations, and that other accommodations are in place if necessary. They do not want him to receive more than he really needs. They believe their boys must be challenged to work hard. She said she doesn't want everything handed to Cameron or her other children. She feels it is all right for him to struggle some so that he won't be afraid to try. Allison knows in the real world you have to work hard to succeed and she wants her children to be prepared. She believes that because many teachers today understand learning differences they are more flexible than when she and Evan were in elementary school. The technology that teachers have in the class rooms today allows them to reach students who have many different styles of learning. Allison especially likes the computers and other opportunities her boys have. The Tracey's have lap tops at home. Because they want their boys to learn how to type, they have typing tutors and games to use in the summer.

As a child, Allison had painful experiences related to school achievement. She does not want her children to have similar problems. She wanted to be like her friends. It seemed to her that they could do math problems easily while she struggled! Many seemed organized and she was disorganized! In third grade the teacher recognized Allison needed help and she was sent to a resource room. However she didn't receive much help there, but by fourth grade it was different. This teacher was wonderful. She made the children feel they were in the right place to learn and they were taught in a different style from their other classes. Allison loved to be there. The teacher was fantastic! She did projects that Allison remembers today. This fourth grade teacher really helped Allison learn what she needed and to feel good about herself.

Seventh and eighth grades were terrible experiences for Allison. She was sent to the resource room, but it was very different from her elementary school experiences. It seemed to her that everyone else in the class had a behavior problem. She did not. She felt frustrated and isolated. She was often the only girl in the class. Today she believes that not only were her problems unaddressed, but also the needs of dreamers or students with Attention Deficit Disorder were ignored. In some cases students with Attention Deficit Hyperactivity Disorder (ADHD) were recognized because they were discipline problems. She was quiet. Most of the class time was spent disciplining the other students; she felt it was a waste of time because she did not learn much.

Tenth grade was different. Allison again had a great teacher who believed in teaching the "whole child." Allison loved her. She knows the teacher tried to help each child believe in himself or herself. Self-esteem had to be one of her goals. Allison remembers this teacher saying if you don't believe you can do it, you can't do it. Believe you can! These are lessons Allison is teaching her children today.

When it became time for college, Allison was fearful. She had been hurt when a teacher told her parents that possibly she should get a GED by passing the General Educational Development test. Her parents disagreed. They believed she could graduate with her class and attend a college that had a supportive program. Wesleyan was the right place for her. She remembers as a freshman being shy and really needing socialization. Her learning disabilities were in math and organizational skills. The friendliness of the campus with people saying hi to her as she walked to class, plus the faculty really seeming to care about her, enabled her to develop the socialization skills she needed. Joining a sorority helped her make lifelong friendships that continue today. Her sorority sisters go on trips together and make frequent phone calls to each other. The study skills course enabled her to develop organizational skills which she tried to use during college and since. The Learning Center became a comfortable place where she could study in the evenings. She appreciated the caring staff. She will always remember June Bracken who would listen as Allison shared how stressed out she was, and just by talking and listening helped Allison calm down and do better. Even during tests, June would allow her to stop, take a breath, and relax before continuing. At The Learning Center, Allison knew no one thought there were "dumb questions" and she was able to receive various kinds of support. Careful advising allowed her to choose the right math classes, explore areas that interested her, and choose courses where she could use her talents.

Allison became an Art Major. This was a turning point in her college career. Previously, she often had periods of highs and lows, but the art classes allowed her to recognize her talents. It was a perfect major for her. The professors in the Art Department were helpful and caring. She will always remember the ceramics teacher inviting the class for dinner and showing them his studio. Her art teachers were positive, allowing Allison to discover her talents and to continue developing a good self-esteem. The highlight was her senior art show which was a combination of all her hard work and was displayed for everyone to see. On this special day all of the senior art majors and families were invited to a reception. This became a time for these students to appreciate each other's work and to think about possibilities for the future.

After graduating from Wesleyan Allison began working at Bloomingdale's Department Store selling sheets. At Bloomingdale's she became very interested in the visual art display department, and as a result she was promoted to a managerial position. Despite her success, she realized this wasn't what she wanted to do all her life. She wanted more opportunities to use her art ability. She quit her job and volunteered at The Lab School in Washington, DC.

The Lab School was known for its work with children who had learning disabilities. Allison was able to do art projects with these children and take them around to various classes. She worked with some graduate students and assisted in the class room. The Lab School was a wonderful place with a great art program. This was a time when Allison was able to reflect on what she wanted to do in life. She now had a goal and knew she wanted to become a teacher.

In the fall she began working at St Patrick's Episcopal School as the director of the Child Care Center. They had an outstanding preschool program which incorporated art in many ways. Since the St Patrick's school was near The Lab School, Allison was still able to do some volunteer work there after school. While teaching during the day, she entered evening graduate classes at Mary Mount College, and began earning a degree in Education with a specialty in Learning Disabilities. Her courses were stimulating and she became excited and focused! She was able to connect her own life experiences as a child with the teaching she was currently doing. She hoped that she could not only teach but also be an advocate for others with disabilities. While teaching and doing graduate work she married Evan Tracey, whom she had been dating for six years.

In high school and at college Allison occasionally practiced with the track and cross country teams. Her goal was to run marathons, and she did run two marathons. She believes anyone can run a marathon, but they have to be determined and disciplined. Running 20 miles was an important goal because the additional miles in the marathon seemed possible after the 20th mile point. Evan helped her in her training by riding his bike beside her as she ran. Team work, determination, and hard work are a part of Allison's personality which she illustrates in all she does. When she began graduate school, she realized she had to change goals in order to teach, study, and have a family. Marathon running would be postponed for the future. Allison realizes she has learned the organizational skills she needs and is able to structure her life and help others including her family.

Allison enjoys her life as a wife and mother. She still creates a few art pieces and especially enjoys doing art with and for preschool children. She is using her education major and teaching background to help her children. She tries to be a good role model and to show them that actions get results. Organizational skills will always be a challenge, but Allison believes when her family works together as a team they will have success.

LAURA OVERLY FISHER

Phyllis Coston and Laura Overly Fisher when she received the award for graduating magna cum laude.

Laura is an ordained Methodist minister and a woman who loves learning, but hated school. Her story illustrates that dyslexics may learn differently, but they can learn and be successful.

Laura's Story

Laura can only remember school as a place she hated. She has a sister two years older and one two years younger who were very smart, enjoyed school, and were loved by their teachers. Laura's parents had no reason to think her experience with school would be any different from her older sister's. After all, Laura enjoyed the books that her mother and grandmother read to her, and she seemed to be able to read them by herself. However, it turned out that Laura had memorized the books, which caused her mother to believe Laura could read before entering first grade. Surprisingly, Laura was placed in the slowest reading group, which made her feel she was stupid. This fear remained with her all through school. Her mother suspected something was wrong when she received Laura's Mother's Day gift, a plaque she had made at school. "Happy Mother's Day" was printed with the *p*'s in "happy" reversed. Her mother joked that it was her "HAGGY MOTHER'S DAY" plaque; but in truth it was the first indicator that Laura might need more than just time to catch up with the other children.

Laura was the only one from the slowest reading group who was passed on to second grade. Laura was told this was because she was at grade level or above in all other areas, including reading comprehension. It was decided that being in the slowest reading group should not hold her back. She was passed to the second grade on the condition that she would go to a special reading class for one hour twice a week. Laura has always thought it was fortunate this was her second grade teacher's last year before retirement. She was a kind lady, and Laura was able to get away without doing the work. For instance, when they did math in their workbooks and Laura's name was called to show her work to the teacher, Laura would pretend she didn't hear her, and the teacher would finally go to the next person. She liked math, but she sat at the back of the class where there were many distractions. She often missed or could not remember what the teacher had said. She could not read the instructions in the book, and was too embarrassed to ask for help. Laura still can't figure out how she passed but is grateful she did.

Laura's favorite class in second grade was the special reading group. She was dismissed to go to a special teacher who had the children sit at a table and discuss the work. She loved learning this way. Laura knows she is an experiential/ interactive learner who does well in small groups. She excelled in this class since the others were very slow readers. She read better and did well in discussions. This helped her self-esteem, as well as being a reprieve from sitting still and being quiet in the regular class.

Each year at the end of summer, Laura cried because she didn't want to go back to school. However in third grade she was challenged in positive ways and was able to use her creativity. In spelling class they were challenged to use as many spelling words as they could in a sentence. This was fun for Laura. Sometimes she even got all ten words in one sentence. Others came to Laura for help. This enabled her to feel she wasn't stupid and had something to contribute.

At the end of the summer when Laura was to begin fourth grade, as usual she was dreading going back to school. She had no idea how awful school was going to be that year! For years her parents shied away from even mentioning her fourth grade teacher's name, because Laura would go off on a tirade of complaints about both the teacher and that year. Fourth grade is a difficult year for many. There is a big transition from third to fourth grade because more content material is presented and more is expected of the students. Laura remembers coming home from school and throwing her book bag in the hall with no intention of opening it to do her homework. She would run to the woods and pretend she was an animal because animals don't have to go to school.

One of her worst fourth grade experiences was enduring reading class. When the whole class took turns reading aloud, if she did not know the word, Laura would often pretend that she had lost her place. Then the teacher would say the word to help her find her place, and sometimes Laura could figure out the rest of the sentences. If one word was not sufficient she would keep pretending to be lost. Sometimes this would be enough to get the teacher to move on to the next student. At other times students tried to help her by pointing out the section in her book. The solution then was to have the book drop on the floor! In most cases the frustrated teacher would move on to the next student. Laura was terrified people would realize she couldn't read and think she was stupid. In her mind it was better to be thought of as being lazy and not paying attention than to be thought of as stupid.

One of Laura's biggest problems was focusing. The words went together when she tried to read, and in math the numbers in the problems moved around. Although she was good in math, her grades in math were always lowered because she reversed her numbers. She would have just focused on her paper to figure out what it said when the boy in front of her would reach behind and move her paper back and forth, which made her lose focus on the page. This caused her to explode out of her seat and attack him. He didn't do it to be mean; he just enjoyed provoking her. She was the smallest kid in the class and he was the tallest. It was quite a sight to see this little girl pummeling the biggest boy, especially since he was laughing the whole time. It seems her teachers were amazed and didn't know what to do. They never told her parents about it until it stopped.

Her dad became more aware of her problems as the nature of her homework changed, and the nature of his work changed. She had to read and write book reports in the fourth grade. Laura and her dad began to read the books together. Sometimes he'd read to her and she would write her book report, which would be full of spelling errors and reversals. Laura's dad worked with learning disabled children in his profession at Family Services. As a result of working closely with Laura, her dad realized she needed help. He recalls that while working on a case with another child, a light bulb went off and he realized, "She is like Laura; I need to get Laura tested!" Her dad took Laura to Akron, Ohio, where she was diagnosed as having a visual perception problem. She was put on Ritalin and also got glasses.

The school principal had not agreed with her being tested as he thought the parents were simply comparing her to her sister, Amanda (who was a straight-A student), rather than accepting that Laura wasn't as capable as Amanda. It is interesting that when Laura heard this, she wrote to the principal that her parents were not comparing her to her sister. (Not many elementary school children would be inspired to do this!) She said in the letter that she needed to know what was wrong with her. She explained that she wanted to be tested and have a tutor so that she could learn to read and be able to read all the wonderful books her parents had in their basement. Her letter was full of reversals. Her mother kept a copy of it for years.

After Laura was diagnosed and her work had improved, Laura's parents met with her teacher at a parent-teacher conference. They received a much better report about Laura's work. Her parents were surprised to learn that she had fought and beat up bigger boys. But they were pleased to also learn that now she was no longer doing this. The teacher who did not believe in learning disabilities credited Laura's progress to her new glasses. Laura's actions were different from many girls with learning disabilities. Boys frustrated by learning disabilities often get aggressive. Girls frequently become quiet and sometimes cry a lot. At times Laura was aggressive, at other times quiet.

Fifth grade was a good year for Laura. She understood she still had a problem, but the Ritalin and glasses helped, as did the one-on-one tutoring. She also began to understand her problems and develop better ways to compensate. She was always about a year or a year and a half behind in her reading level. Her comprehension scores were high but the vocabulary section was very low. Her spelling scores were low as she continued to reverse letters. Laura was above average in math, usually on the 90th or 99th percentile. She said it was easier to get along in class when you are on the third grade reading level in fifth grade than on the second grade level in fourth grade, because of the nature of the reading material. This is a good observation. In Laura's case, her comprehension level was good, which certainly helped her succeed. She was also assigned to a tutor, which meant she left the classroom for one hour, twice a week to get one-on-one instruction. She always excelled in those situations which gave her a reprieve from the stresses of the classroom. Laura stated:

> "I give the tutors I had in elementary and high school a lot of credit for understanding that sometimes the most constructive way to spend the time was just to let me vent my frustration over what was happening in the classroom and with my teachers. Sometimes I would just lay on the floor and cry or scream. Of course they also did a great deal to help me improve my reading, class work, and self-esteem. I owe them a great deal."

Sixth grade was not a good year. Laura and the teacher did not relate well to each other. Laura became frustrated when she was thrown out of class, so she decided to go to another sixth grade class. The teacher of the second class was willing to accept Laura, but the principal would not condone a student changing classes in this manner.

Laura thinks it was around eighth grade when she was visiting a friend and learned that her friend's brother was dyslexic. She asked what that was. They told her it meant that he saw things backward. Laura says she thought, "Big whoop! If I just saw everything backwards I could just learn to reverse things." Laura's problem was that the letters would not stay in the same order. For instance, she remembers studying spelling in elementary school. She was sure the word she had to learn was spelled "Firday" because that was what the book said. She knew from patterns that the spelling would more likely be "Fri" rather than "Fir", so she re-checked the book and again saw "Fir". Therefore that became the way she learned it and wrote it on the spelling test. When it was marked wrong, she decided to show that teacher her book to prove she had spelled it the way the book did. She was shocked that her book now said "Friday". Bewildered, she wondered what the point was in studying if you studied it wrong.

Laura now believes it might have been helpful if she had received more systematic help with Phonics. Teachers and tutors tried; but Laura had no concept of how to sound out words. She would get the sounds in the wrong syllable, leave sounds out like she did with letters, or would start the word with the strongest sound, rather than the first sound. She also remembers when she asked a teacher how to spell a word they would instruct her to look it up in a dictionary. Laura said, 'It was so frustrating. Do you have any idea how long it takes to find a word in the dictionary when you don't even have the first three letters correct? I don't think I would have ever found "***enough***" trying to spell it "***nuff***". Even today computer spell checkers often have no idea what word I am trying to spell." (Author's recommendation: The Franklin Speller is a better help with this problem today than computer spell checkers.)

Reversing numbers works the same as reversing letters for Laura. She remembers when she had to use a phone with a rotary dial; she would dial many times before getting the number sequence correct.

She could use a push button phone more easily because she learned patterns for the sequence of numbers rather than trying to remember the numbers. Patterns worked well for her.

The way things moved around for Laura, she would get something right one time and get it wrong the next time. Teachers who did not understand her problems often accused her of being lazy, uncaring, or not careful enough. Laura used to get angry with her teachers who did this, but now she has much more sympathy for them as people who wanted to help her learn but simply didn't know what to do. Every method they tried didn't work. Most of her teachers probably went to school when little was known about dyslexia, and some didn't believe it existed. At the time, she just thought they were mean and incapable of listening or caring. She now believes the teachers were as frustrated as she was because they did not know how to help her.

Laura feels she was fortunate because her parents were willing to say, "We don't know what's going on. We need help!" This allowed Laura to say, "I don't know what's going on. I need help." Her parents took her places to find ways to meet her needs. Her parents discovered early on that one of Laura's greatest fears was that she was stupid. They did a lot to make her realize her problem was not about being stupid. They told her that you can't be classified as being Learning Disabled if you don't have the ability to learn the material; otherwise you would be classified as something else. Laura said, "My parents went out of their way to emphasize that I was smart. This was good for me to understand because it was really important to me to be smart."

Laura explained, "My mother and grandmother were avid readers. My grandmother was a school teacher, with a college education, which was unusual for a woman born in the early 20th century." By fifth or sixth grade Laura was able to read adequately, but she still loved to have her grandmother read to her, particularly reading challenging material such as *The Chronicles of Narnia*. Her grandmother also played learning games with her. Probably as a result of her grandmother's and mother's interest, Laura is an avid reader today, even reading faster than many of her peers.

When Laura was in fourth or fifth grade, she remembers her parents taking her to a learning center specializing in learning disabilities. They wanted to discover how she learned and how they could help her learn. The final report said Laura had taught herself to read. This amazed her parents who were very quick to encourage Laura to learn—**her way**!

When Laura was in seventh grade, one of her teachers was finishing her Master's Degree and planned to do a paper on a gifted student. She chose Laura. Since it was so important for Laura to be smart, this was a big deal for her. Laura never had the opportunity to read the paper until she was a junior in high school. Her teacher had written that Laura had dyslexia. Previously she just knew it as a visual perception problem. Her parents had known she was dyslexic but were surprised that they hadn't communicated this to her.

In twelfth grade, Laura decided to write her senior paper on dyslexia. She became fascinated in learning what dyslexia was all about. When she discussed her paper with her parents, they told her that she had taught herself to read and to spell, and that her vocabulary was memorized. This helped her realize why her teachers were so frustrated with her. They would tell her to look at the word and sound it out. But the word she saw would scramble, and she would have to close her eyes or look at the ceiling and pull it from her brain to find the word.

When I asked her to explain this procedure, she told me I had to understand what happened to her when she got mono in her junior year in high school. It was as if she had a stroke. She lost all her compensation skills. She could not read, spell, write, or even copy a math problem from a book. She said that she was just so tired and frustrated; she felt she was back in first grade, and it was terrible. She identifies with her friends who have had strokes when they tell her that they know it is all there, but they can't get it out.

When writing a paper, Laura would stop and say, "How did I do this?" She would look at the ceiling and turn to the right, then she would close her eyes and pull the word out of her memory.

I asked Laura to tell me the steps she used to understand her letters. She reminded me that her compensation skills went out the window when she had mono. She had to rethink what she did. She said, "I had to be intentional at what I did. I had to close my eyes and go to my brain file until I found it in my memory." When she found words, which might be reversed, she then analyzed them. To her, every letter in the alphabet has a face. An *L* had a face that went to the right and an *a* had a face that went to the left. She explained:

> My name is Laura, so my first two letters faced each other. Most letters in the alphabet are like *L*, and only a few are like *a*, so I memorized those letters. I remembered in kindergarten my letters had faces on them. Remembering this helped me. My letters would walk. *L* would go walking to the right and *a* to the left. I had to spell on my fingers to write my letters. I also couldn't write a + (addition) sign, and the x (multiplication) sign wouldn't lay right. It was awful, but it was also wonderful. I am one of the few dyslexics out there who had to learn my compensation skills in a way to become aware of them. I know some of the things are automatic, and I would never have known them if I hadn't had mono. I didn't have one bit of energy to compensate for them. I enjoyed sharing this in college in a presentation on dyslexia in an education classes. The teacher asked me what could be done for students like this. I said the most important thing is to keep the sense of hope and motivation there."

After graduating from high school, Laura began to look at colleges and was accepted at West Virginia Wesleyan. Before entering college, she had hated school; college was much more enjoyable. She felt there were reasons for this: the size of the school, the professors, and the choices of classes. She believes she had more opportunity for gaining knowledge because college fit her style of learning. For her, high school was too structured. College presented the right balance. There was structure without rigidity.

Laura felt the advising process at the Learning Center was very helpful. When I met with her, we discussed her learning style, the teaching style of the professors, and her best time of day for taking classes. We weren't always able to be successful in meeting these needs, but often succeeded. Laura wanted to be an "A student", but usually found that she couldn't make straight A's during a semester. She usually made one B and planned in advance which would be her B course. This choice was usually based on the amount of reading and number of papers required, as well as her interest in the subject. She appreciated professors who wouldn't allow her to use dyslexia as an excuse for spelling and other errors but insisted she use the proofreading services of the Learning Center. She was the first student in our program to graduate Magna Cum Laude.

Laura was positive about her Wesleyan experiences, particularly her opportunity to study under the late John Warner, chair of the Sociology Department and an ordained minister. Dr. Warner developed a Youth Service major designed to prepare students to work with youth especially in social work or church vocations. Laura took many of the classes from the Youth Services major for her major in Sociology. She also minored in Christian Education. These were classes she enjoyed and they became helpful to her. During the summer between her sophomore and junior year in college, she married Joseph Fisher, a ministerial student at Wesleyan. They have had a good marriage.

After graduation from Wesleyan, Joe and Laura attended Emory Theological Seminary. During her last semester at Emory, she became pastor of a small church. She enjoyed the members and had a good experience.

Following graduation in 1994 from Emory, Joe and Laura returned to West Virginia where they both served small churches. Laura faced the problem of not being accepted by some members because she was a woman. This was disappointing, but not unusual for women clergy at this time in history. She continued in her ministry. Laura was ordained a Deacon in the United Methodist West Virginia Annual Conference in 1996.

Laura and Joe accepted the opportunity to serve on the staff of a large church in Florida. She discovered that working on a staff in a large church seemed to be her calling. It gave her an opportunity to be part of a ministry team and to work with small groups where she excelled. She was able to use her background in youth services and Christian Education as well as her creativity. Since she was an Associate Pastor prejudice against a woman in ministry was less pronounced.

After two years they were appointed in 1998 to serve smaller churches in North Florida. Joe enjoyed the pastorate, and the people enjoyed him. Laura again faced some discrimination because she was a woman. She was ordained Elder in the United Methodist Florida Annual Conference in 2002.

Joe had a dream to be a chaplain in the Military Service. Since he was nearing the age limit for applying and Laura wasn't happy at her church, they agreed Joe should apply and he was accepted as a military chaplain. Laura felt it was the right time for her to travel and to think through her calling. She took a voluntary leave of absence in order to be able to travel with Joe. He has been stationed in a number of interesting locations, including England. Laura has enjoyed opportunities for traveling and learning. Recently they returned to the United States and are living in Phoenix, Arizona, where Joe is stationed. Laura is still working through what God is calling her to do next.

Laura's Tips

1. Encourage creativity, and help people find what learning styles and environments work for them.
2. Give permission to make mistakes without it being seen as failure.
3. Focus on how people learn differently, and celebrate it, rather than focusing on learning disabilities.
4. Don't miss the forest for the trees; express your idea first before getting lost in spell checking and other details.

ISAAC WILLIS

I saac had a dream to become a basketball coach. His father had a dream that Isaac would be a doctor. Isaac fulfilled both dreams!

Isaac's Story

Jeremiah 29:11 "For surely I know the plans I have for you, says the Lord, plans for your welfare and not for harm, to give you a future with hope." (New Revised Standard Version)

Isaac asked that I begin his story with this scripture verse from the Bible. It has been extremely important to him on his life's journey. Isaac is a dedicated Christian and his faith in God has enabled him to succeed in life.

Isaac had very supportive and outstanding parents who helped him succeed. He is proud of his parents. They began college at ages 15 and 16 at a time when few African Americans attended college. His father also graduated from medical school, becoming a renowned dermatologist. His mother pursued graduate studies and received a PhD.

Growing up in an environment where academics were constantly stressed wasn't easy for Isaac. He had many painful experiences along the way. Not only did he realize how intelligent his parents were, but also his brother was outstanding in school, becoming a graduate of Harvard and eventually a doctor as well. On the other hand, as a young boy, Isaac was a "daydreamer" and often a failure. He even recounts one time as a youngster while playing little league baseball, he was asked to play first base at practice. However, he ended up daydreaming and remembers being hit in the head with the baseball.

In elementary school Isaac's love for sports began and playing sports meant a great deal to him. His parents were supportive, but he had to keep a good grade point average. The result! Isaac was dropped from the baseball teams and the football teams several times because of grades.

Junior high years are often difficult and this was especially true for Isaac. He attended a private school through the eighth grade. However, because of a history of low academic achievement, Isaac was put on academic probation. Things still did not improve and eighth grade was a disaster. He had numerous academic problems as he was failing many subjects. By this time, he had become so used to failing, that he began to view D's as "good grades" and aimed to achieve them. Finally his academic record was so bad that he was kicked out of the private school.

At that time the only option seemed to be attending ninth grade in the public school. This was a dramatic "eye opener!" He didn't receive any help, and his social life suffered as well. On one occasion, he was even held at knifepoint. His parents realized something had to be done and he transferred to Woodward Academy, where he received several tests. The tests revealed two things: Isaac had a very high IQ and had a learning disability. This meant he could succeed, but needed special help.

Transferring to Woodward Academy in 10th grade was the right approach. The school, which had previously been a military academy, had become a co-ed academy. Here, Isaac received a life changing educational experience. Thelma Ridgeway, a wonderful teacher, took Isaac under her wing. She prepared an IEP (Individual Educational Plan) for him. She knew what he needed and he finally was able to experience a "TASTE OF SUCCESS!"

Because Woodward Academy was a boarding school, it gave Isaac a structured environment which was what he needed. After supper each evening there was a supervised study hall where he received needed help. Isaac said that he became an "academic animal" after tasting success and found himself always wanting to learn more and make higher grades. Isaac said that while in elementary school, he had gotten to a point of wanting to make D's instead of F's—now he was striving to make A's all the time. He made the honor roll, something he had never experienced before. It was a thrill! He was not only proud, but also his parents were proud of him. Since his home was only 30 minutes away, he could go home on the weekends, allowing his parents to recognize his feelings of success.

In 12th grade he began playing basketball and fell in love with it. He was not a polished offensive player, but played extremely good defense and was a great hustler. Playing basketball made him realize the importance of self-discipline. By this time, he had developed time management skills in order to make good grades.

The three years at Woodward passed quickly and he was ready for college. He was still a dreamer and dreamed of playing college basketball. He especially wanted to attend Syracuse University in New York, a school known for good academics and basketball. He was accepted and attended Syracuse, but the difference between Woodward Academy and Syracuse University was dramatic! He immediately joined hundreds of other young men to try out for the one spot open on the basketball team. The competition was great and he was not chosen. Having been used to small classes, he was shocked to attend his first chemistry class in a huge room filled with 600 students watching the professor on a large TV screen. Unfortunately, despite the fact that he was struggling academically, it was also disheartening that he did not have access to professors as he did in high school. As a result, he failed!

His mother began searching for small schools with supportive programs. As a result he visited West Virginia Wesleyan. After his interview, he felt Wesleyan was the right place for him. However, he hated leaving his friends and after having bad experiences, it wasn't easy to try again. He remembers crying while riding on the small commuter airplane from Pittsburgh, Pa to Clarksburg, WV. He said it seems strange, but the ironic thing is that he remembers crying again on the plane four years later going home after graduating from Wesleyan. It was hard to move on from so many great experiences and friends.

He was thrilled at Wesleyan when as a walk-on, he was chosen for the basketball team. Isaac loved the coach, respected the staff, cared deeply for and supported his teammates. He gave his best to both the team and his academics. He often made the dean's list throughout his college career and had one of the highest Grade Point Averages' on the team.

He attributed part of his success at Wesleyan to people who cared and supported him. He knew his parents were rooting for him. The coach not only helped him improve as a player, but also encouraged him to succeed academically. Isaac compared me to his teacher, Thelma Ridgeway. He said I encouraged him and he believed I loved him. Teachers can make a difference! It was thrilling for me that, at his last basketball game as a senior, Isaac wanted me to present his trophy. Isaac is 6'3" and I am 4'11". When I gave him the trophy and he bent over to kiss me, the people in the stands laughed and applauded. They were all proud of Isaac, the team's captain, and the team's accomplishments. This team had compiled a record for the most wins in four years in the school's history and had captured the West Virginia Intercollegiate Athletic Conference championship that year, 1991. Isaac graduated with an Adult Fitness Major and a Nutrition Minor. He was not certain of his future plans. He considered physical therapy or occupational therapy. However his Dad's passion was for Isaac to become a doctor. Isaac appreciated his parents so much and wanted to please them. This, of course, meant medical school.

Although Isaac had taken a great many science courses, he did not have Biochemistry or Physics which were requirements for medical school. During the next two years he attended Morehouse College, taking these two courses and studying for the MCAT exam. He was not accepted into medical school the first year he applied. He began teaching Physical Education in a High Point Elementary School while he continued studying.

Isaac was accepted into medical school the following year. In 1994, he began his medical career in Philadelphia at The Pennsylvania College of Podiatric Medicine. Medical School was difficult. At Wesleyan part of the reason he was very successful was his photographic memory. He realized he had to go beyond his memorization ability for the higher level medical courses. New ideas were coming at him so fast and he needed an in depth understanding in order to succeed. Exams were torture. Isaac also realized he did better with hands on experiences rather than straight lecture courses. This recognition caused him to transfer to California College of Podiatric Medicine in San Francisco.

He graduated in 2000 and was ready for his residency, which was granted by New York College of Podiatric Medicine. He was appointed to Long Beach Medical Center in Long Island, New York. He felt blessed because immediately he met Arnold Horowitz, who was in his second year of residency and helped him learn "the ropes." They quickly became very close friends. They often worked night shift and early morning rounds together.

On the evening of September 10, 2001, he watched Monday night football never dreaming of the change that would occur in his life the next day. As he was doing his rounds the next morning, 9/11, a nurse came in and said a plane had hit the New York trade center. He still was not aware of what this meant. Arnold came to the room and said, "Come with me immediately. New York is being attacked and my wife is in the city." He tried frantically to reach her on his cell phone with no success. He wanted to drive to his house to use the land phone. Isaac went with him but remained outside and had a good view of New York. He watched as the first tower collapsed, followed by the second. They had to return to the hospital as wounded would be arriving. Arnold was almost hysterical. He still could not reach his wife, and it would be days before he knew she was alive. Isaac empathized and supported him.

The following day Isaac volunteered to go down to Ground Zero to be part of a triage unit. They met at a historic church in Manhattan. It was a time he will never forget. He recalls that it was like entering another world. It was extremely gloomy and ash was everywhere. Although he had a mask, his eyes burned and his nose began to run as soon as he got out of the car. In the midst of this he was concerned for his landlady. He knew that she worked downtown, so he was worried about her safety. He was relieved when she reappeared at home days later. I asked what he remembered most. He said, "I never saw such love shown by others from all over the country. I was impressed with all of the volunteers at the triage unit who came from all around the country to do anything at all just to help. There were also signed banners from Oklahoma and other states that were raised throughout the balconies of the church. It didn't matter what color of skin you had, everyone wanted to help and genuinely cared. To be completely honest with you, as a minority person, I was surprised that I felt absolutely no racism! Everyone waved as I walked or ran down the boardwalk, there was a look that said, 'I need you.' Racism within the United States of America became very petty because everyone was threatened all of a sudden. From this tragedy we drew closer together."

Isaac also talked about walking by the hospital where he saw pictures of victims and missing people. As he looked at their faces he remembered Sept 10th when he was watching Monday night football, and wondered how many of these people were also watching, spending time with loved ones, or simply walking their dogs for the last time. He said, "I realized how blessed we are to have the life we have. These were people my age, younger or older."

A week later, another tragedy occurred when a plane crashed in Long Island. The chaos was a lot smoother this time, perhaps due to all of the events from the previous week. As Isaac was making his rounds on patients this time, he could clearly hear across the speaker in the hospital that a request had been made for all doctors and nurses to go to the plane crash site. Public transportation was halted. Passengers were removed. Doctors, fireman, policemen and other emergency workers were allowed to immediately board. Isaac was very quick to respond and he was one of the first doctors to arrive on the scene. At that time they did not know if this was another terrorist attack; but instead, it turned out to be a tragic mishap. The plane not only crashed, but also landed upon a few residential homes as well. Therefore, lives were at stake within the plane and the homes. As Isaac arrived, he noticed that one of the plane's engines had landed at a gas station, which would have been even more traumatic if it had landed on the gasoline pumps.

The experiences at Ground zero and at the plane crash have become lasting memories for Isaac. As he has thought about how worried his mother was because she couldn't reach him, and his own worry about his landlady and Arnold's wife, both of whom were stranded in Manhattan for several days, he realized how vulnerable we truly are and how much we need each other and, most of all, need God.

The events of 9/11 occurred during Isaac's second year of residency. As he began thinking of his next step of graduating and setting up a practice, he was asked if he would consider becoming chief resident for the residency program. This meant another year of residency, but the opportunity was one he felt he couldn't refuse. He had good experiences during his residency, but his love of basketball was always with him. After their 48 hour shifts ended, his friends went home and collapsed; but he would turn on the TV to watch basketball games. He recalls that prior to one game in particular when he imagined what it would be like to address his team with the pre-game speech, he found himself pacing around his apartment as if he were talking to the team. Then suddenly, he laughed and said to himself, "What are you doing? You just finished being on-call and you're up here dreaming about coaching." He couldn't seem to get basketball out of his system. The only family member with whom he shared his passion for basketball was his brother, a surgeon. His brother understood, and told him he thought that he would be a great coach.

During that time his mother had a recurrence of cancer. When he had been in eighth grade, she had been diagnosed with cancer. He remembers his fears of that word, "cancer." She had been in remission for years, but now it had recurred. His fears for her life were great, and on July 1st, when his third year of residency had ended, he flew home to be with her. His mother and grandmother had been his greatest fans. He wanted to be at home and take care of his mother. She had been so supportive of him and helped him succeed. He really wanted to help her. His birthday is on October 4th, and he recalls her saying that they would celebrate his birthday when she felt better. Unfortunately she died ten days later on October 14th. Death does not destroy love, and on her birthday each year no matter where he is living, he makes the trip to the cemetery to place flowers on her grave.

Isaac shared with me that he knows people respond to grief in different ways. This was true with him and his father. It was decision time for Isaac. His father assumed that he would begin his career as a Doctor of Podiatric Medicine. However, Isaac still had his dream of coaching basketball. He had always followed his parents' wishes, which was why he had gone to medical school in the first place; but he didn't believe he wanted to practice medicine all of his life. Basketball was his love.

His brother, who understood Isaac so well, was in favor of Isaac pursuing his dream of coaching. Since he was a family member, he seemed to understand Isaac's dilemma. He even gave him $7,000.00 to help him find a place to live for the following year. Isaac still feels that the only way he was able to break the cycle of doing only what was expected of him was that it was a family member who told him it was all right to pursue his dream. At this time, Isaac and his father became estranged. His father, who was an army colonel with a military background, expected his sons to respond to him the way soldiers did. Isaac had always responded this way; but this was his future. He believed that this estrangement was a clear indication of what would continue if he did not do what was expected. At this crucial time in his life, following the death of his mother and because it was vocational decision time for him, he needed the support of his family.

Isaac's Christian faith helped him realize that he had to follow his passion, but also he believes it was God's timing. A job coaching a basketball team did not open immediately. However, following his mother's death, he had time to really reflect. He drew nearer to God, which allowed him to place himself and his future into God's hands. Should he seek the security of money and open a medical practice, or would opportunities eventually open for him to coach? As summer approached he knew he had to take the initiative by following his passion for basketball and seeking some type of position. His hope was a college coaching job. He didn't realize exactly how competitive the pursuit of a collegiate coaching job would be. His first decision was to attend as many collegiate summer camps as he could. During the summer, he was able to coach at the Paul Hewitt Basketball Camp at Georgia Tech, the Jeff Capel Camp at Virginia Commonwealth University, and the Jim Larranaga Basketball Camp at George Mason University. All of these were great opportunities to gain coaching experience. However, it wasn't until the very end of the summer while at George Mason, that he met someone who knew of a coaching vacancy at Lycoming College.

He pursued this lead, and interviewed for the position. He was thrilled when he was hired. Since Lycoming College was a Division 3 level athletic program, Isaac was the only assistant coach. Among other responsibilities, not only was he to coach but also to help recruit. They were particularly interested in recruiting minority students. He recruited eight players, seven of whom were African American. One of these recruits became "Rookie of the Year." This ended up being the most diverse class in Lycoming History.

Isaac coached at Lycoming from 2004 to 2006. He enjoyed his experience there, but he wanted eventually to become an assistant coach at an Ivy League School. He heard of a possible opening at Brown University and pursued that lead. He was successful and joined the coaching staff there in 2006.

Isaac felt coaching at Brown was fulfilling his dreams. Even more important, one of his most memorable experiences was when he looked out at the stands and saw his dad sitting with his brother and sister-in-law, rooting for him and the team. He was thrilled as he and his father spent time together later and he realized his father seemed to understand that Issac had to follow his dream. The following year his father died. Isaac truly loved his father and appreciates all he did for him.

Isaac is proud of his part in helping Brown have their best single season record of 19 wins, and a second place finish in the Ivy League. While he was on the staff, the team also had a trip to the Inaugural College Basketball Invitational Tournament.

Isaac really enjoyed his two years (2006-2008) at Brown. He is especially proud that four of his student athletes graduated and went on to play professional basketball. Although he enjoyed coaching at Brown he felt that when the head coach left, it was time for him to move on also. He had experience being an assistant coach. He asked himself, "Am I ready to be a head coach?" He heard of a position in Pasadena, California at the California Institute of Technology. He decided to pursue it. After a two week process, he was one of two finalists. Unfortunately his lack of head coaching experience was probably against him, giving the other person the position.

Isaac and I share the belief: "When a door closes, God opens a window." The window opened and he was asked to join the staff of the Basketball Training Institute in Pasadena, California. He enjoyed his time there with student athletes and parents, and was very successful.

After two years, Isaac felt God's nudge. He realized he was being called to return home to Georgia to build his own basketball program that would glorify God. He followed God's call and became the founder and CEO of the Christian Basketball Academy in Atlanta, Georgia.

The two goals of the Christian Basketball Academy are:

1. To help students develop into well rounded student athletes who have a firm foundation in God.
2. To develop these student athletes into individuals who can compete at an elite level, both academically and athletically.

Isaac feels blessed that he now has the opportunity to help others. He is also ever so grateful for his parents who supported and loved him on his journey. He said he had the best parents in the world, and could not have succeeded without them. They were truly a blessing. He thanks God for them!

It seems only proper to end Isaac's story with the verse with which I began. This verse is extremely meaningful to Isaac as he seeks God's leading in his personal journey: "For I know the plans I have for you, says the Lord. They are plans for good and not for evil, to give you a future and a hope." Jeremiah 29:11 (The Living Bible)

FRED CONKLIN

Fred Conklin is a successful attorney today, living in Smyrna, Georgia. Fred is a partner in the law firm of Cuzdey, Ehrmann, Wagner, Stine, Sansalone and Bobe LLC. He is married to Brenda Orr, also a graduate of Wesleyan, where they met. They have two fine boys, Jack and Grayson. The Conklins enjoy family times together.

Fred Conklin's Story

Fred recalls in elementary school he was known as being messy. His desk and papers were always unorganized. There were papers on the floor all around his desk. This upset his teachers, and they admonished him in a negative way because he would lose his homework and other papers. At that time no one in education sought a reason for his disorganization. "This is just the way Fred is!" He needed to try harder. The teachers talked to his parents about his disorganization. His parents tried to help, but were unable to succeed. Later when he was a teenager, he was tested for a learning disability and the results of these tests indicated he had a learning disability which affected his focusing and concentrating. At last this helped explain why he seemed to have so many things going on in his brain at once. This kept him from paying attention to his work, papers, etc.

Fred said that as he progressed in school, the lack of organizational skills was always with him. In high school his teachers often told him that he had a high IQ and great potential, but he didn't work up to it. However, he remembers a bright spot. He had a wonderful high school math teacher, Mr. Chandler, who inspired him and used humor in his teaching. This made the class came alive! Fred was able to pay attention! He realized he was not only learning but also enjoying math even though it was never a favorite subject. He was thrilled to receive an A. Fred said: "This was the first time I began to learn the importance and utility of identifying the best way for me to learn a particular subject; more specifically, how I could force my mind to absorb a particular subject. The "traditional" way subjects were being taught did not work for the way my mind worked. I realized for the first time in Mr. Chandler's class that I could make a subject fun, or look at it in a different way, and it would actually stick in my memory bank. That was a real turning point for me!"

Co-curricular activities are always important in school. Fred was interested in music. He enjoyed playing the drums in a rock band in high school. He also played piano and guitar. Playing tuba in the high school marching band was another pleasure. He enjoyed music more than his other classes. In many of his classes he had problems focusing, concentrating, and often was bored. The result: he just squeaked through them.

After graduating from high school, Fred was expected to go on to college. He was accepted and enrolled at Clemson University. He felt fortunate to be accepted because his high school career was nothing to brag about. He said he and his parents were pleased there was a center for people with learning disabilities on campus. He agreed with them that he needed to use it. When he went to the center, he was disappointed. The "help" he was given turned out to be two pamphlets for him to read: one was on "How to Study" and the second on "How to focus." Fred needed more help than this as he wasn't ready for college. The first semester classes were tough, but "the social life was great." However, the fun came to an end! He was put on academic probation and later asked by the college to stay out of school for a semester before applying to return.

After receiving the letter from Clemson telling him not to return, it was time for a "heart to heart talk" with his parents. They told him they loved him, but were not willing to pay for college for him to have fun and not study. His parents began talking about other options including the military. His mother had done research and discovered Wesleyan's Special Support Program through a neighbor whose son was enrolled in the West Virginia Wesleyan College Learning Center. He said his talk with the neighbor and family was like "an altar call." His parents were impressed with Wesleyan' services, but knew Fred had to become a serious student. In a sense this was his "last chance." When I studied Fred's application materials, I was impressed that he had a great deal of potential; but I knew he would need to use the services of the center to succeed.

Fred wanted to please his parents and definitely wanted to succeed. He did use the learning center services! In fact, Fred enjoyed his time there so much that he became a student assistant in Wesleyan's computer lab. In reflecting on his experiences in the center, he said that he is so grateful for the time management course which not only helped him in college and graduate work, but continues to help him in his work today. He is usually able to complete his work at the office and have time to spend with family which is important to him.

Fred said as he thinks about his time at Wesleyan, he realizes the Learning Center was at the cutting edge of technology. Wesleyan had the first computer lab on campus with staff to give help. (Later, Fred himself helped others as a student assistant in the lab.) Fred particularly appreciated recorded books. Hearing the words and seeing them helped with his concentration. He said the tools that he was given at the center helped build his self-confidence and it was those tools that gave him the knowledge that he could succeed in law school.

Dating his wife, Brenda, also helped him become a better student. Brenda was an outstanding student and studied regularly. If he was going to date her, he had to get his act together and study. They met for the first time, and spoke briefly when Brenda came into the computer lab to work on a paper. She asked Fred for help with a word processing program, and he was immediately taken with her. They were able to get to know one another better while both of them were working on the play, *Kiss Me Kate*. Brenda was an intern in the box office through the Accounting Department (accounting was her major.) Fred had agreed to help a friend who was the House Manager by volunteering as an usher. He and Brenda worked together at the theatre for three days, and then began dating. Fred had never gone with a girl who was studious and interested in academics. Studying with her helped prepare him for law school, and he knew that if he wanted to convince her to marry him, he would have to grow up and work hard to succeed in life. He wanted the best for Brenda and he knew that meant that he would have to make the best of himself by harvesting his full potential.

Brenda graduated in 1991, but Fred stayed an extra semester graduating in 1992. They were married on September 19, 1992, in Brenda's home town, Clarksburg, West Virginia. After they were married they both worked saving money for law school. Fred was accepted at Michigan State University in 1996 where he studied and worked hard, graduating in 1999. Brenda worked on her "PHT" (putting hubby through) as an accountant in a large East Lansing accounting firm, making law school affordable. Law school is tough, but Fred worked hard and did well. In addition to his studies, Fred was a team Captain and Brief Writer for a number of the competitive traveling moot court teams, and was privileged to be on the Moot Court Board, where he served on the Executive Committee. These teams participated in mock trial competitions. One of his teams, in fact, placed in the Stetson International Environmental Law Moot Court Competition in Houston, Texas. It was a great experience and helped prepare him for his career today as a trial lawyer. Fred is certain that the skills he developed with the help of the Learning Center were key to his ability to handle such a difficult undertaking successfully. Fred was also honored to have been elected by his fellow law school students as President of his graduating class.

After graduation Fred and Brenda moved to Fred's home town, Kingsport, Tennessee, where he passed the bar and began his practice. They spent about a year in Kingsport. Then a couple with whom they had been friends at law school encouraged them to move to Atlanta, Georgia. They did. Fred joined the firm of Cuzdey, Ehrmann, Wagner,

Stine, Sansalone and Bobe LLC. They still live in the Atlanta area and Fred is a partner in the firm today.

When I talked with Fred about interests and activities, he shared that he still appreciates music. He and his oldest son, Jack, go to afternoon concerts together. Jack really enjoys music. He plays the standing base in the school orchestra and also plays the guitar. In addition to his music interests, Jack is a catcher on a little league baseball team and the family likes to go to the games and cheer him on. Fred's younger son Grayson is very artistic and expressive. These are talents Fred and Brenda strongly encourage him to pursue.

The Conklins have a family tradition of attending Camp Falling Creek in western North Carolina near Asheville. This is the camp Fred went to as a child and through high school. While in college, he worked there as a camp counselor during the summer vacations. His boys now love being campers for several weeks during the summers.

Fred appreciates the people who have supported him in his life's journey. He particularly mentioned a neighbor who helped him when he was "messy Fred." She didn't concentrate on his disorganization. She helped him realize his positive traits and helped him build his self-confidence. He will never forget her. His parents were always there for him and help him in many ways. Fred said, "I couldn't have made it without my parents." He added, "Most important to my educational development, however, was the staff of the Learning Center, especially Dr. Coston. I never would have made it through college without them. Moreover, what I have learned from them about studying and working efficiently, I have carried with me into my career as an attorney."

Fred shares the following tips which he hopes will be helpful to others.

1. Take full advantage of technology. There are many devices and applications that can be used throughout your life to help you study and later, as an adult, to do your job effectively and efficiently.
2. Don't be afraid of recorded textbooks. These are among the most important time management tools.

3. Use the spell checker.
4. Don't be discouraged. There is always a way out, and there is always a way to do things that will work better for you.
5. Learn from other people's mistakes, and train yourself not to make those same mistakes.
6. It is important to pay attention to how those around you learn, and do not be afraid to emulate those techniques. Find what works for you by paying attention to those around you.

ANDREW COLLINS

Can a dyslexic become a doctor? Andrew Collins proved that the answer is yes! Dr. Andrew Collins is a podiatrist whose office is in Lewes, Delaware. He also has privileges in several hospitals in Lewes, Delaware; Rehoboth Beach, Delaware; and Philadelphia, Pennsylvania. It took hard work, supportive parents, and caring persons along the way for him to reach this goal.

Andrew "Drew" Collins' Story

Drew attended elementary and high school in the 1970's and 1980's when little was known about learning disabilities, and many pupils who learned differently were looked down upon by teachers and other children. He remembers moving around to various schools, often because of unhappy experiences. He now realizes his parents were trying to find the right school for him.

Since he was having a great deal of trouble in fourth grade, his parents had him tested early in the semester and discovered he was dyslexic. After searching for a new school that could meet his needs, they chose Beachwood School. Here the class size was six pupils and two teachers who focused on a variety of learning issues. This was the right place for Drew as he not only received the help he needed, but also felt comfortable. It was a safe place. He knew the teachers and administrators liked him and wanted to help him succeed. Since the school only went through sixth grade, he had to change schools for seventh grade.

He spent seventh grade at Upland County Day School where they understood dyslexia, and he received special help which included untimed testing and tutoring during a special study hall. The classes were small with fifteen students per class and thirty students per grade. Participating in sports was required. As a dyslexic he still had times of frustration and found sports to be a valuable outlet. In addition to the mandatory three sports, he found Tae Kwon Do Marshall Arts to be very helpful in setting goals, helping him focus, and building his self-confidence.

The next step in his educational journey was attending Sanford High School, a small private school with fifteen to twenty students per class and a graduating class of thirty-eight. Untimed testing was the primary accommodation given. He was main-streamed for all his classes. They did not have tutors, but his mother tutored him daily. He continued his Tae Kwon Do Marshall Arts which helped relieve his stress level.

Throughout school his mother was his greatest supporter. Although she worked all day, she spent 4 to 5 hours each evening helping him. He said, "She was the most influential person in my life. Without her help, I would not have achieved." He remembers her saying, "If you know you have tried your hardest and did your best then you can be proud of yourself. You can only be sad if you didn't do all that you can, and that is something you have to live with."

Before beginning high school, his parents had him retested by a special doctor. The doctor wrote his parents telling them not to send him to college but to a technical school. His parents disagreed with this. They had faith in him and knew he could succeed. They did not tell Drew about this letter until he had successfully completed his freshman year in college, proving the doctor wrong. His parents were helpful in his search for the right college. Together they looked at many colleges but discovered most offered very limited support. Drew realized that the support given at Wesleyan was exactly what he needed. Although he wanted to attend Salisbury State because of the surfing and other fun activities near his home, he knew Wesleyan was the college for him.

Drew appreciated the Learning Center staff and many of his professors. He shared that Dr. Herbert Coston, who gave oral exams, made it possible for him to make A's on tests in the History of Western Civilization. With the help of his Learning Center tutor he discovered that practicing his answers to the essay questions by tape recording his answers, helped him share his answers easily with Dr. Coston. Dr. Hamner and Dr. Capstack, both in the Chemistry Department, were also very helpful. Dr. Hamner made chemistry come alive. Each class was challenging but entertaining. Dr Capstack was always willing to give advice about graduate schools, etc., and he became Drew's co-advisor with me.

Drew's vocational dream was to be a doctor, which requires a great many science courses. However, he discovered he enjoyed and did well in many liberal arts courses, especially art classes in which he had a minor. He particularly enjoyed Ceramics and Sculpturing. It seemed appropriate to pursue a Bachelor of Arts in Science with a major in chemistry, rather than a Bachelor of Science Degree. He had to be sure he met medical school requirements when making this decision.

In Drew's junior year, it was time to begin thinking of medical schools. He shared with me some of his dilemma. He wanted to be a doctor, but wasn't sure which field of medicine to pursue. I told him to apply to a variety of medical schools and to choose the one that accepted him. He applied to podiatry, chiropractic, and dentistry schools. I called all of the schools and discussed his dyslexia because many medical schools weren't aware of the strength and potential of dyslexics. Several months later he returned to my office to share the good news that he had been accepted into all the medical schools to which he had applied. He still had the dilemma of choosing the best field for him. Since his father was a pediatric orthodontist, one brother and several cousins were chiropractors, and a close friend of his sister was a podiatrist, I suggested he spend some time with each of them. He found podiatry different from anything he had been exposed to, and it fit his interest and ability. Podiatry also gave him opportunity to do surgery which was a big interest to him.

Graduation time approached and he needed to take a few courses in summer or fall to meet all of his requirements. It was important that he participate in the May graduation so his mother, who had cancer and only a short time to live, could be there. Everything was arranged for him to participate; but his mother died a month before the graduation ceremony. This was sad since she had worked so hard to help him reach this goal. It was both a happy and difficult time for Drew and his family.

After finishing his courses, Drew realized that medical school would be more difficult than college. He was accepted into a special summer program to prepare him for the challenge. His greatest obstacle was the heavy course load. An accommodation recommended to him and some others was to spread the first year's courses over a two year period. This was the right decision for a dyslexic as it made the reading load manageable. His other accommodation was the opportunity to have untimed tests. He also subscribed to a note taking service which was available to everyone. Lecture notes were transcribed for all courses. He found his third and fourth year with heavier course loads to be very difficult, but he managed them and particularly enjoyed clinical and intern work where he had hands-on experiences. During his fifth year where he had externships, he was able to explore residency opportunities.

Residency is very competitive and challenging, and the period of waiting to be chosen to the right one was stressful. His desire was to get as much surgical experience as possible. He was accepted and did his residency at hospitals in Brooklyn, Harlem, and Long Island. In Long Island he worked 80 hours a week which included 10 hour days and a 34-hour shift every third day. It was both a challenging and great experience.

Because of his interest and desire to get as much surgical experience as possible, he pursued more residency training. The first was in an operating room unit where he had many surgical opportunities. The second was an offer from the Dean at Temple University School of Podiatric Medicine to work in North Eastern Hospital. After the first six months, a special surgical position was offered to him making him chief of the podiatry residents in the Surgical Residency Program. Through these opportunities, he was able to fulfill his dream of having many surgical experiences and he became a graduate of The Surgical Residency Program.

After completing these residency experiences, he had several opportunities to work in Pennsylvania while preparing to set up his own practice. He believes that setting up his own practice was his most terrifying experience. He appreciated his father's advice and financial help in making this possible. He began his private practice in Lewes, Delaware, in 2004. It was a long journey to reach this goal. Drew worked hard and appreciates the support he had along the way.

Drew's Advice to Young People or Others with LD:

1. The only thing shameful is not trying.
2. Never put yourself down.
3. It is okay to fail if you have tried.
4. Don't put up with "What ifs." (These are obstacles to achievement)
5. Follow the Nike commercial: "Just Do it."

TOM MERRILL'S GUYS: JAMIE FLUKE, GREGG MCFARLAND, AND JIM CHIANG

1992—Thomas Merrill

During the school year 1984-85, I went to a conference in Connecticut to learn about the Macintosh computer which was relatively new. It seemed to be an answer to writing and spelling problems so common among dyslexics. We ordered a number

| 65

of these and began the first computer lab on campus. Margery Richter who was in charge of our Learning Center Laboratory added supervising computer use to her already busy job.

The computer was so helpful for the LD students that we had to expand. We created a separate computer lab and in 1988 we hired an Assistant Director, Thomas Merrill. He not only knew computers but also had the right personality and skills to work with students and supervise the lab. Tom, a recently retired army colonel, had been a chaplain. He not only knew how to teach, but also to listen. He became loved by the students, especially the student assistants he trained. He gave them freedom to run the lab. He taught them that freedom carried with it responsibility and empowered them to live up to their potential. This teaching enhanced their self-esteem. Those who were especially competent supervised the lab in the evenings, Saturdays, and Sundays. For this book, I have selected three students who went on to careers using computers. In interviews, each one told me they were doing everything Tom Merrill taught them.

Jamie Fluke's Story

Jamie is dysgraphic, which means he cannot cope with handwriting. Since he had faulty control of his muscle system used to encode letters and word forms accurately, his writing was illegible. Unfortunately he had teachers who couldn't distinguish between this perceptual problem and carelessness. Insensitive teachers told him that he was lazy; others told him he would never get anywhere. His third grade experience was so painful that he has blocked it from his memory. No one even thought of a learning disability.

He remembers elementary school was difficult. He did not understand why he seemed different from other kids. He recalls that in each new grade with a new teacher, he got through the first grading period fairly well because his intelligence hid his disability, but as the year went on his teacher became increasingly frustrated with his achievement level. In those days, before teachers were aware of learning disabilities, if a student did not achieve it was usually assumed he was either stupid or lazy. Jamie's teachers tended to assume lazy because they could see he was not stupid, and made comments to him accordingly. In sixth grade he remembers a teacher was giving him such a hard time that he walked out of the room. She probably was trying to motivate him, with comments such as, "I don't understand why you are not getting the work. Are you just lazy?" Jamie knew he was really trying, not being lazy. When he began to cry, left the room, and walked around the building, he went to his mother who was a teacher's aide in the school. His mother talked with the teacher, but Jamie was very upset by the incident. At that time his parents knew there was some kind of issue with his learning, but they had no idea what it was.

Six months later Jamie's mother read an article about Albert Einstein's dyslexia, and showed the article to him and his father. They all agreed, "That's Jamie!" Identifying the problem was the first step toward really dealing with it by giving it a description and the name, dyslexia. Now he understood. He really could say, "I'm not crazy! I understand what's wrong. Other people have it and can deal with it. I can too!" Then his parents had him tested at A I Dupont Children's Hospital, and the diagnosis of dysgraphia, a specific form of dyslexia, was confirmed.

The second step of Jamie's turnaround involved both healing the past and developing his coping skills. He went through about two years of counseling to restore his self-esteem, after years of self-doubt and teachers' criticisms. He developed his use of the computer as a coping device by getting a Commodore 64 computer. The computer was not new to him as he started using a computer when he was about 10 years old, mostly to play games. He enjoyed it, and now he quickly recognized it as a coping skill. He was using a word processor long before his peers. Most people were still using typewriters or just writing. He said, "I would have been 'dead in the water' if I had to depend on writing."

Jamie sees the third step preparing him for success as the confidence he gained in a nine week summer program for dyslexics at Landmark School, between his junior and senior years in high school. Some of the courses were helpful, but the true value of the summer to him was in realizing his problems were not insurmountable. He said, "It was more a mental thing, not an educational thing. It was a self-awareness and reevaluation of me." He met other students like himself, and some whose problems were even worse. He felt lucky that at least he could read; some of them could not. He finally became really confident that he could and would succeed at a level he desired. He would just ignore the Guidance Counselor back at his high school who recently had told him, "I don't know why you're applying for college; you'll never get in."

After the summer he was offered the opportunity to participate in an outstanding Watermark program which meant traveling around the world having learning experiences as a senior at Landmark. But he chose to return to his high school because he wanted to be mainstreamed and graduate there. He had friends in his high school, and he loved being in the marching band. He was determined to prove himself. Jamie's marching band experience illustrates the confidence he had gained in the summer, as well as the determination which always characterized his actions. Since he had missed band camp, he had to learn all of the music and field maneuvers for the show in just over two weeks. He had not been put into the lineup with the other trombones, so he had to be the only trombone at the end of the formation among other instruments, and he had no support there. That took confidence! He is proud not only of how well he did in the shows that year, but also of how his fellow band members recognized his determination and achievement.

Junior and senior high often were not good experiences. He still had to be thick skinned and take criticism. Along with criticisms were comments trying to get him to "be more realistic", as several teachers continued to tell him not to apply to colleges because he would not be admitted. These teachers told him to set new career goals. Jamie and his family did not agree.

In the fall of Jamie's senior year I was attending a conference in Philadelphia. After the conference I interviewed Jamie and his father. I was impressed with Jamie's determination and desire to succeed. I encouraged him to visit our campus to see if it was a right fit for him. He applied for our program and was accepted. He was one of the first students in his high school class to receive an acceptance letter from a college. I had expedited his acceptance after being so impressed in our interview by his great determination. When he told a Guidance Counselor he had been accepted at W. V. Wesleyan, which she knew was a good liberal arts college with selective enrollment, she did not believe him until he showed her his acceptance letter.

As a freshman at Wesleyan he was enthusiastic about his classes. He loved his history and psychology classes. He had been a prime candidate for Dr. Herb Coston's Western Civilization history class, because Dr Coston gave everyone the chance to take oral exams. Jamie didn't have to get bogged down with writing his answers; he could share them orally which he loved doing. Around midterm time, he asked me if he could be a tutor for Western Civilization. We usually did not have first semester students tutor, but because of his eagerness and Dr. Coston's recommendation, we granted him this opportunity. He was an especially gifted tutor. He developed a strategy for another LD student who had problems writing. Jamie recommended the student prepare answers to essay questions using a tape recorder. This worked! Jamie and his tutee both earned A's in the course. Others began requesting Jamie as a tutor. This did wonders for his self-esteem.

Working in the Learning Center computer lab under Tom Merrill was Jamie's greatest college experience and prepared him for future careers. In addition to the Learning Center staff, he commented that he was really helped by Dr. Mike Choban and Dr. Richard Calef, psychology professors, and Dr. Herbert Coston in history. He said, "They had faith in me." He graduated with a double major in history and psychology. He chose psychology because he felt it would enable him to help future students, and history because he loved it.

After graduation Jamie worked at the Xerox Company, The Internet Service Provider Company, and is presently at Penn State. Jamie loves the irony: as a young man he was told he could never be accepted as a student at Penn State but now he is an administrator there. He is Network Print Systems Coordinator. His duties include management of all the high speed production printers (100 pages a minute or more) and also the network infrastructure to which these systems connect.

Jamie is happily married to Kim who works with LD children and teens. He has opportunities to help her by sharing his early frustrations and feelings which he hopes will help others. Kim and Jamie are now foster parents. They believe their foster son is LD; Jamie can hardly believe the similarities of his son's problems with his own at the same age. Because of red tape, getting his foster son tested and their suspicions confirmed by the school district has been difficult. They plan to have him tested privately. Jamie says his tip about support (see below) has become prophetic, as he and Kim have become their foster son's support system.

TIPS FROM JAMIE:

1. You have to have a support network. If it is not your parents, you have to find someone else.
2. If you don't have support you may never reach your goal.

Gregg McFarland's Story

Gregg McFarland, a 1992 West Virginia Wesleyan College graduate, was an outstanding assistant in the Learning Center computer lab, often working week-ends and evenings handling the lab without a professional supervisor. Gregg is now using his computer skills as Microcomputer Technician specializing in Macintosh computers for Data Management Services. His story is very different from Jamie's. Although dyslexic, he did not seem to have as many frustrations and bad experiences in school. He was not diagnosed until he was in tenth grade when his teachers and parents realized he needed to be tested.

However, he did have several painful experiences. In junior high when he was planning his high school curriculum, his counselor suggested he should be enrolled in shop and a curriculum which was not pre-college. His parents advocated for him, agreeing with Gregg's desire for the college prep curriculum. Trying to convince the school system he should be in college prep courses was a frustrating experience but in the end he was placed there and did very well. Another painful experience was needing to ask for help. He is an independent person and asking for help was always difficult.

When it was time for college he looked for schools with special programs. Wesleyan provided coping skills rather than emphasizing remedial work. Since his problem was reading textbooks, recorded books were the answer for him. He still struggled with understanding math concepts, but tutors were helpful.

When asked about his best experiences in college, the number one experience was meeting his wife, Trish. He hung out with her and friends in his freshman year and went steady with her beginning in his senior year. The second experience was his special internship at Sea World. The third was the Learning Center, especially his work with Tom Merrill in the computer lab.

Tom encouraged the assistants to trouble shoot and was not harsh if they went on tangents. There was a lot to learn, as this was the time the hard drive was just beginning to be introduced to supplement or replace the old floppy disk system. Tom and the assistants worked together, learning in a friendly and encouraging atmosphere. Tom's style and his teaching methods have helped Gregg in his vocation today.

As a communications major, Gregg found his internship at Sea World was a wonderful learning experience. This independent study allowed him to use their video and audio equipment. He worked in the editing department, and especially enjoyed the auditory department, preparing sound effects for shows. As part of his work he prepared a video to show potential employees who were entering the entertainment field. For Gregg this was a dream come true.

After graduation he worked in the audio department at Sea World. It was fun not only hearing but also being the squeaking door. However, after working several years, he followed Trish to Washington DC where he had several jobs until he found a position as an internet provider.

Today Gregg is a family man enjoying his wife, Trish, and two daughters, Ellie and Lydia. Trish, who is also a Wesleyan graduate, enjoys working in a lab testing drugs on cancer cells.

Jim Chiang's Story

Jim Chiang is a businessman who has worked hard to achieve success. He was helped by Tom Merrill, the Assistant Director of the Learning Center, to develop computer skills which he still uses today.

Jim's disability is auditory processing, making it difficult at times to process what is being said. However, he has learned coping strategies to enable him to be successful. He has had both positive and negative experiences in school. He had good learning disability teachers in elementary school and junior high. It was in high school that he experienced greater challenges. Jim felt his high school LD teacher just wrote him off. She didn't feel he should or could attend college. He was given no help, only discouragement about taking ACT and SAT exams. The teacher told him that he should find some type of work after high school since she didn't believe he could succeed in college. Although he was hurt, Jim didn't accept her opinion, nor did his parents.

Jim's parents supported his desire to attend college and arranged for special tutors to help him. He was fortunate because one of his tutors knew a counselor at another high school who worked with learning disabled students, especially helping those who wanted to attend college. This counselor was willing to meet with Jim after school and she helped him prepare for ACT and SAT exams as well as recommending colleges with LD programs that he should visit.

Jim followed his counselor's advice and visited several schools. He and I met and we had a good interview at Wesleyan. I was sure he could be successful. He was happy to spend time after our interview with Dr. Herbert Coston, Chairman of the History Department. History was Jim's love and he and Dr. Coston clicked! Jim was accepted at Wesleyan, and attended a College Preview Day where Dr. Herbert Coston spent over an hour helping him select the "right schedule of classes." Jim did have a good first semester. He said that having Dr. Coston as an academic advisor as well as one of his professors was very helpful.

The study skills class in the learning center was particularly useful his first semester. In this course he appreciated the Myers Briggs Type Indicator, which helped him understand his personality type, as well as other inventories that helped him understand himself and his learning style. Discovering that he was a visual learner was helpful in selecting courses for the second semester. He and his advisor chose professors who wrote on the blackboard and/or used an overhead projector so he could see as well as listen to the lectures. The time management unit in the study skills course helped him especially to learn to focus and prioritize things. He is certain that the emphasis to focus on your strengths and not your weaknesses helped him in college, and that same emphasis helps him today. He believes that the friendliness of Wesleyan's campus and his caring professors contributed to his having had a successful college career.

Among the caring people who enriched Jim's life was Tom Merrill, Assistant Director of the Learning Center and Supervisor of the Computer lab. Tom asked Jim to become a Student Assistant. Jim said he will never forget this opportunity because it was a great learning experience. He is a "hands on" learner and by helping others, he helped himself. Tom was impressed that Jim was a very responsible young man, and chose him to work some evenings and weekends when Tom was away. Jim says he has used the skills and the work ethic he learned from Mr. Merrill in his career today. He also credits this work with giving him leadership ability not only in relation to the computer but also with helping him develop skills in working with others. He believes his church and Wesleyan helped him develop a good self-esteem.

After graduation, Jim had several positions. He worked in a bookstore and in a medical facility using the computer skills he had learned at Wesleyan. He decided that while he was young and not tied down with a family, he should learn more about his heritage. His parents were originally from Taiwan, and he decided to go there. This was a great experience which changed his life. In February 1999, he went to Taiwan and lived with his relatives. He began teaching English as a second language. While teaching he met many young people whose friendships he enjoyed. After completing his teaching experience, he knew he must return to America to begin his career. In 2004 he enjoyed returning to Taiwan for a friend's wedding, giving him opportunities to renew his friendships there.

Religion is important to Jim, and he attends church and small study groups. He believes his faith has helped him cope with his disability, be successful in his career, and live a meaningful life.

Today Jim is married and has a son of whom he is very proud. He lives in northern Virginia and works with a small company that finances utility companies in rural areas. He finds his work very rewarding. He particularly likes working with his manager who is a Christian and supports Jim in whatever he does. His manager has given him many opportunities for learning, speaking to him as an equal and not talking down to him. Jim said, "When I use my computer skills, I often remember Tom Merrill and his wonderful spirit as well as his helpfulness."

Jim recommends the following tips for students today:

1. Don't give up, no matter what other people say.
2. You may hear you are lazy, dumb, etc., but remember we all have strengths and should focus on them.
3. Don't think about failing, but focus on succeeding.

Tom Merrill reached many students and his philosophy of life and caring manner contributed to their success. The stories of Jamie, Gregg and Jim represent only a few of the students with whom Tom worked. The computer has been a wonderful tool and has helped many with learning and physical problems succeed.

DIANE LEO MENORCA

Diane Leo Menorca is a 1992 graduate of West Virginia Wesleyan College. After graduating from Wesleyan, Diane pursued a master's degree in International Relations and has had a career in government in Washington DC. She has not allowed dyslexia to prevent her from achieving her goals in life.

Diane's Story

Diane was a happy preschooler who enjoyed life. Her grandfather was so proud of her, and often commented on how smart she was. Everyone agreed. She even walked and talked early. Therefore, it was a shock to the family when she did not do well in first grade. In fact, her parents were stunned to get a note from the principal at the end of her first year saying that she would be "placed ahead," even though she had failed to meet the requirements of the first grade. In the second grade Diane continued having "great difficulty" with reading. Her parents were distressed and could not fathom what the difficulties were.

In the spring of her second grade, her mother attended a conference sponsored by the Suffolk County Orton Society and heard Dr. Nina Traub speak on "How to Recognize a Learning Disabled Student." Dr. Traub had developed her own version of the Orton-Gillingham method of teaching dyslexic children how to read.

As Diane's mother was listening to Dr. Traub's lecture, suddenly everything became clear. Diane was a very bright, but dyslexic child. They took that information to the principal and staff at her school, but they were shocked to learn that the public school had no programs at all for the remediation of learning disabled children. For the balance of Diane's second grade, Diane dictated little stories to her mother who would then type them up and then Diane could "read" them to her classmates and thereby participate somewhat in her last few days of public schooling.

At the recommendation of Dr. Nina Traub and the President of the Orton Dyslexia Society, Diane's parents had her tested by the Language Clinic at Massachusetts General Hospital in Boston. Dr. Samuel Orton, a pioneer in the study and treatment of dyslexia, had begun that program in the 1930's.

The diagnosis Diane received from a pediatric neurologist in the Language Clinic was "developmental dyslexia." This diagnosis did not seem to be taken seriously by the principal and the staff at her public elementary school. In 1978, the public schools had not yet begun to understand learning disabilities, despite the fact that they were required by recently enacted legislation on both the federal and New York State levels to provide "individualized" programs to remediate LD students.

Diane's parents decided to enroll her in a nearby private church affiliated school known as the Emmanuel Lutheran School. This school had a basic understanding of dyslexia because the principal of the school had a brother who had severe emotional problems as a result of his own un-remediated dyslexia.

Diane did very well during her four years at Emmanuel Lutheran School. She had regular classes and was mainstreamed with all of the other students, but went to a language lab for one period each day. In the language lab she was taught to read by a multi-sensory approach introduced by the Suffolk County Orton Society. Diane's best friend was in the Gifted Student program and also attended classes at Suffolk College. Diane had four very happy and successful years of elementary education. At her sixth grade graduation Diane was presented with the "Christian Citizenship" award, given to the student showing outstanding character.

Diane's parents believed that she would continue to do well in middle school at a similar private school. They were disappointed, however, with her academic progress because the school did not have the appropriate supportive programs or language lab. They then enrolled her in eighth grade at another local private boarding and day school which advertised that it specialized in remedial programs and individualized attention. She did well academically, and was active in the equestrian program, winning several awards. It soon became apparent, however, that Diane was missing out on the "boarding experience" in a very small community of students. As she was approaching the end of eighth grade, her parents were advised by close friends from the Orton Society that if boarding was necessary, Diane might enjoy The Forman School in Litchtfield, CT where their children were students.

During this time Diane's mother, Joyce Leo, became an active member of the Orton Society, now known as The International Dyslexia Society, which offers research, teacher training, parent education, and state and national conferences to help people understand dyslexia. Mrs. Leo became president of the Suffolk County branch of the organization and worked hard to introduce multi-sensory training to all of the 72 school districts in Suffolk County. The organization offered teacher training classes during the summer months and advocated alterations in the public schools in teaching dyslexic students. The Society also collaborates with the Harvard Medical School's Neurology Department's on-going Dyslexia Brain Research Project documenting neuronal differences in the ways dyslexics experience the world.

Diane attended The Forman School in Litchfield, CT for her entire four years of high school from 1984 through 1988. As painful as it was for Diane's parents to send her to a school far away from home at the age of 13, it soon became apparent that Diane and her parents had made the right decision. The Forman School was, and continues to be, an outstanding college preparatory school for dyslexics. At The Forman School Diane began using the Macintosh Computers in the Language Lab and began realizing that they significantly improved her reading, writing, and comprehension.

During her four years at Forman, Diane developed academically, and accelerated in social, athletic, and leadership skills. She was on the school soccer team, the volleyball team, and the softball team during all four years, winning several MVP and Sportsmanship awards. During her senior year Diane was given "The Outstanding Athlete of the Year" award, and at graduation she was given the Headmaster's Award for Quiet Service, for recognition that she contributed "greatly to the life and the welfare of the school," in a quiet and unassuming manner. She also received the E. D. Hale Award, given by the Learning Center of Forman to the student who had achieved the most "commendable progress through diligence and perseverance."

Many learning disabled students go through stages similar to some of the stages of grief: denial, anger, recognition and acceptance. Diane's years in school with other dyslexics helped her accept being dyslexic without going through all the stages of grief. Being dyslexic did not seem like a "big deal." Some of her best friends were dyslexic. She only remembers one experience that highlighted the misperception that some people have about dyslexics. As a young adult Diane fell into conversation with someone who happened to be from Litchfield, who said, "I can't believe you went to that school for stupid kids." Diane let this misguided comment roll off her back, because she knew that dyslexia has nothing to do with intelligence.

Diane said that even after that experience, she has always talked freely about her disability. However, she has discovered that she doesn't need to mention it, and most people are not aware she is dyslexic. She said it is really an invisible condition not obvious until the person is faced with reading or writing.

During her senior year at The Forman School Diane applied to and visited several colleges, including West Virginia Wesleyan, in order to select the best fit for her. The program at the Emmanuel Lutheran School convinced Diane and her parents that West Virginian Wesleyan would be an ideal college for her in that she would be main-streamed, yet have a supportive learning center available for her.

On a spring day in 1988, Diane and her father flew to West Virginia Wesleyan where I interviewed them. Diane was very eager to learn as much as possible about the college and it's Learning Center. The interview and the campus visit made West Virginia Wesleyan Diane's number 1 choice. One of her close Forman classmates joined her in coming to Wesleyan.

Although Diane and her family believed that her four years at Forman had prepared her for college, they were impressed with the fact that at Wesleyan Diane would be mainstreamed in her college courses, but would be able to attend classes and tutoring sessions at the Learning Center as often as was required and/or needed. This type of main-stream challenge combined with support as needed was similar to the programs she had received in her previous schools where she flourished.

Diane arrived on the Wesleyan campus in the fall of 1988, and quickly made new friends and began making academic progress. She also played on volleyball and soccer teams. She joined Alpha Delta Pi sorority which provided her with most of her extracurricular activities, because the sorority sponsored many charitable and social events throughout her college years. Today a number of those West Virginia Wesleyan graduates get together regularly in the DC area where they live and work. In 2012, Diane attended the 20th Reunion of the Class of 1992 on the West Virginia Wesleyan campus. Here she again enjoyed being with many of her college friends.

Upon graduation in 1992, Diane and a close group of her Wesleyan friends flew to London, visited Paris, and then toured Europe on a Eurail pass. At the end of the summer of international travel, Diane began graduate work at Central Connecticut State University in New Britain, CT where she obtained a Master's Degree in International Relations. The highlight of Diane's graduate work came in the summer of 1993. This was an opportunity sponsored by the university to study abroad in China, Japan, and Hong Kong. During the trip Diane was even offered an opportunity to teach English in a Chinese rural area.

After graduation Diane moved to Washington DC., taking a hostess position with the Congressional Country Club. Her first government position was as a staff assistant to newly elected Congressman Michael Forbes of Long Island, New York. Diane remained with Congressman

Forbes for three years and worked as a legislative correspondent in the office of Congressman John J. Duncan, Jr. of Tennessee. Later, Diane accepted a position at The Hospitality and Information Service (THIS) of Meridian International Center, an organization which welcomes diplomats and their embassies. In 2000, Diane returned to Capitol Hill to work in the office of Congressman Dan Burton. In 2001, Diane had the opportunity to be in the House Gallery for President George W. Bush's speech on September 20, in the aftermath of the September 11 attacks. After serving as legislative assistant, she rose to the position of Executive Assistant and Office Manager, serving Congressman Burton for 12 years, until he retired in January of 2013.

During these 12 years, Diane made several fact-finding trips on behalf of Congressman Burton, including trips to Morocco, Taiwan, and South Korea. The highlight of her visit to South Korea was a tour of the Kaesong joint industrial zone which extended into North Korea, a rare example of cross-border economic cooperation and a source of hard currency for impoverished North Korea. Diane managed to purchase some North Korean wine for her parents.

During her years on Capitol Hill Diane played intramural softball on the National Mall where she met a fellow congressional staffer, Doug Menorca. They were married in 2002, and live near Capitol Hill with their son, Samuel, and pug dog, Shortstop. After Congressman Burton's retirement, Diane decided she would prefer a part-time position which would enable her to spend more time raising her preschool son.

For years during her government service, Diane also served as a Big Sister to a bright, young girl from an underprivileged background. In 2000, she started a mentoring relationship that blossomed into a friendship which has lasted up to and including today. This young girl is now in college. In 2007, Diane was presented with the "Washington DC Big Sister of the Year Award" at a large dinner attended by the mayor of Washington DC and several high level government officials. Not only did Diane give an acceptance speech, but also the mother of the young girl gave a speech thanking the Big Brother and Big Sister Organization for bringing Diane and her husband Doug into her life and the life of her daughter.

Diane has coped with her dyslexia and realizes life has many challenges. She has given the following tips which she has found helpful:

1. Work hard, never give up.
2. When you are humiliated or frustrated, be patient with yourself and others.
3. Believe in yourself. Don't let others define you.
4. Read about successful Dyslexics. If they can make it, so can you.
5. Keep your self-esteem. You are good at something, even if it's not reading or math. Focus on the good.
6. Find what your gifts are and pursue them. We all have gifts. You have gifts, as well as limitations. Focus on your gifts as you strengthen your weaknesses.
7. Use technological support whenever possible, such as spell checking, audio books, speech writing.
8. Read books and watch videos, such as "Where There's a Will, There's an A."
9. Place yourself in the front row of a classroom so you're more motivated to pay attention and your teacher can see you trying.
10. Above all, enjoy the journey.

PAUL VIRANT

Paul Virant is a nationally known chef whose first restaurant, *Vie*, is a 5 star restaurant listed in the USA Gayot guide of the 40 top restaurants in the country. Paul states, "Whatever the day or immediate need, the *Vie* experience is about providing pleasure and delivering impeccable food and service."

Paul Virant's Story

Paul majored in Nutrition and minored in Biology at West Virginia Wesleyan. After graduating in 1992 he attended the Culinary Institute of America in Hyde Park, New York. The Culinary Institute was a great experience. Following graduation, he worked as a line cook in Manhattan starting at the bottom to learn all aspects of restaurant work.

In 1996 he moved to Chicago where he had various opportunities to work in a variety of restaurants including Trotters. When he moved to Hinsdale, a western suburb near downtown Chicago, he and his wife felt the charm and warmth of this area. They realized it was a great location for a restaurant. In 2004 they opened the *Vie* Restaurant in Western Spring, Illinois. (*Vie* means life in French.) It is a restaurant dedicated to providing a dining experience where one feels pampered and comfortable. Paul said, "I wanted to create an extension of my home, where people can come and enjoy good food in the company of people about whom they care. I want them to enjoy every morsel and drop of life." In 2011 he opened a second restaurant, Perennial Virant, located in Old Town, Chicago.

Being a successful chef doesn't happen overnight or simply as a result of good professional educational experiences, especially if one has a learning disability. Paul's interest and love of preparing foods began as he watched and helped his mother and grandmothers prepare food. It was fun being with them and he recognized their skill and enjoyment in preparing foods. His grandmothers taught him the craft of preserving fruits and pickling vegetables, skills he uses today and teaches others.

Life for Paul was not always successful and enjoyable, especially in school. His learning disability caused problems in reading; he needed extra time and structure in order to read well. Many of the teachers were not supportive or sympathetic to students who learned differently. However, he remembers one teacher, Jim Schute, who was always there for him. Paul said, "He had a great shoulder to lean on." Since Paul stuttered, he worried about speaking as well as reading in front of his class. He took a speech fluency class in ninth grade and his fluency improved greatly; but at times he still stuttered.

Paul's parents and grandparents were always encouraging and helped him develop a good self-esteem. His parents talked with him and together they decided he needed to find a college with a program to meet his style of learning. Although his home in St. Louis was far from West Virginia, Wesleyan's program seemed to meet his needs. There he would be able to take his tests untimed, reading assistance was available, and tutors would help when needed. Most colleges and universities did not supply these in the 1980's before the Americans With Disabilities Act was passed in 1990.

Paul began as a business major which seemed logical to him as his father was a successful business man. During his first year, he learned business was not for him as he did not enjoy the courses. He realized he did not want to follow in his father's career footsteps although he admired him greatly. When Paul and I talked about a career, I asked him what he enjoyed doing. From our conversation I felt he should think seriously about Nutrition major. This was not an easy major because it required many science courses, but he was eager to try. When I introduced him to Dr. Lillian Halverson, the professor for many of the nutrition courses, they really clicked and he was eager to begin. Dr. Halverson and I remember his taking Nutrition 1 and 2 at the same time, which is difficult and unusual, but it was necessary because of starting late in his major. He was so excited when he passed his first test that he left the building and ran to his room to call his father. He was very disappointed when he didn't reach him but came to see me to share the good news.

While in college, Paul worked part time with Dale Hawkins who is currently a well-known West Virginia chef, but at that time was owner and chef of Culinary Creations, a small restaurant outside of Buckhannon. Dale was the ideal boss and this was the ideal place for a creative person like Paul to begin.

Today Paul is not only a renowned chef and owner of two restaurants, but is also a good husband and father. His wife, Jennifer, is a physician of Internal Medicine and a huge support for Paul. Their two boys, Lincoln and James, enjoy family activities such as walks in the woods looking for mushrooms, which is a family tradition.

Paul gives the following tips for young people today:

1. Develop the attitude, "How can I make this succeed."
2. Discover your passion and go for it.

LAURA ROGERS ELLIS

Laura Rogers Ellis is a graduate of West Virginia Wesleyan College. As a small child, it was difficult growing up with a learning disability. Then that six-letter word, *cancer* was added to her challenges!

Laura "Laurie" Rogers Ellis' Story

Laurie was diagnosed with cancer when she was four. She had one of the most common forms of cancer that strikes the young: acute lymphocytic leukemia. The diagnosis was confirmed by a painful bone marrow test. Fortunately a new experimental treatment looked promising. She was lucky enough to enter a trial at the National Institutes of Health (NIH) near her home in Washington, DC. Doctors there told her parents that if this had happened even two years earlier this treatment would not have been available, and she would have only lived for six weeks. Now they held out hope.

The treatment consisted of intravenous chemotherapy, high-dose cranial radiation, monthly bone marrow aspirations in the pelvic bone, and spinal taps. It all worked, and she went into remission. For a hospital, where her oncologist carried her piggy-back down the hallway, NIH was a wonderful place because she spent so much time there. It was almost a home away from home for the next three years. Laurie, one of the first survivors of this newly successful treatment protocol, was the subject of news articles in *The Christian Science Monitor*, as well as *U.S. News & World Report*.

Laurie remembers her mother telling her that many people were praying and rooting for her. Her whole church prayed for her each week. One woman still tells her that she is her hero.

In addition to her physical problems, Laurie had learning problems. In third grade, she began going through the stages of dealing with her LD which are similar to the grief stages. She became frustrated and often angry because she had trouble memorizing, and in science and math she had difficulties grasping formulas. She was frustrated that she couldn't calculate numbers in math in her head or on papers. She knew something was wrong.

Her problems in math became worse by sixth grade. She remembers feeling horrible that she couldn't learn pre-algebra no matter how hard she tried. She sought help from a teacher who didn't understand her problems but told her she was "STUPID." Her experience with this teacher was devastating. She felt miserable, frustrated, angry, and unhappy. Her parents and doctors understood her problems and had her tested for a learning disability. Tests verified that she did have a learning disability—a serious deficit in math caused by her cancer treatments and shared by others who had undergone the same regimen. At that time she was in a private school, but her parents transferred her to a public school which didn't expect all their students to learn at the same rate. This was the beginning of her recognition and acceptance of her learning disability and its impact on her educational career. She worked hard and succeeded. In high school she was in upper level courses in all but math and science.

In her senior year, she interviewed at West Virginia Wesleyan College and was accepted. But in the summer of 1987 after high school graduation when she was planning for college, disaster struck again! Her cancer returned! She had to start treatments immediately, making it impossible for her to attend college as planned. This did not stop her. She is a person with a great deal of resilience and she was able to bounce back. After a year, she entered Wesleyan in 1988. She stayed on chemo for two more years and was treated both at St.

Joseph's hospital in Buckhannon, West Virginia, and by her doctors at NIH. Because the chemo made her feel so sick, she was not able to take a course during the January term her freshman year. During her college career, she spent many mornings before class getting chemo at St. Joseph's Hospital, and the cancer remained in remission. She didn't have enough hours to graduate with her class in the spring of 1992, and this was a big disappointment for her. However, she did graduate in January 1993, which was a great accomplishment. Many students with a learning disability without physical problems take five years to graduate. (Nevertheless, she still considers herself part of the class of '92; she only missed by a month.)

Despite the difficulties, Laurie insists that there have been some remarkable events in her life. One of the most memorable occurred just before she applied to Wesleyan: a challenging summer course with Outward Bound in the north woods of Maine where she found strengths she didn't realize she had. She climbed rocks, portaged canoes, swam in freezing water, spotted several moose, and battled biting black flies. She came through like the proverbial Timex watch that "takes a licking but keeps on ticking."

Laurie remembers fondly the day she was accepted at Wesleyan. She had been visiting other college campuses and had just arrived at one of them in Maine when she asked a student what they did for fun. His response, which left something to be desired was, "We climb a rock wall." Needless to say this was a huge turnoff. Coincidentally, at the time Laurie and her mother were pulling up to Wesleyan's Admissions Office, they received a phone call from her dad. He was calling to let them know that she had been accepted to Wesleyan. At this point, Laurie did not even want to have the interview, and asked her mother if they could turn around and leave. However, she didn't leave. She enjoyed the interview and felt Wesleyan was the right school for her. Today she has many fond memories of college and the friends she made there. She says that she owes her education and friendships to the school and the people in it.

Laurie was in college when she finished chemo for the second time as she was turning 21. She still remembers when her Zeta Tau Alpha "sisters" threw a party for her and presented her with a surprise cake that said, "Congratulations! You did it!"

Despite having to deal with treatments almost on a daily basis, Laurie enjoyed her time at Wesleyan where she majored in studio art and minored in psychology. She particularly remembers her psychology professor, Dr. Richard Calef. His classes were so interesting that she never wanted to miss them. She will always remember her graduation day. When she received her diploma, Dr. Calef winked at her, and it made her feel so good. He knew her struggles and her motivation.

Laurie is talented and has had a variety of jobs since graduation. She has worked in a day care center, has been an administrative assistant in two law firms, was employed in a political public relations firm, and has been a software librarian for the Army National Guard and Defense Security Services. She had to leave a project assistant job because she had a mini-stroke which doctor's felt was a result of her radiation treatment. Again her resilience enabled her to bounce back. Laurie got a call from her project manager at the Army National Guard in October 2010. She had to leave her position there in 2008 because of a contract change. She was thrilled to hear, "It seems your old position has opened up again and we would like to have you come back." Laurie is now back with the Army National Guard in the Configuration Librarian position she had to leave before. It is exactly where she wants to be.

In 2005 Laurie married Richard Ellis, a six-foot tall patent examiner who is a math whiz. Laurie is four-foot nine. She has kept in contact with many Wesleyan friends. One of her best friends from college, Karla Smith, was a bridesmaid, and they see each other often. Another great experience took place on her honeymoon in the US Virgin Islands. She had always wanted to swim with dolphins and finally got her chance.

At home in Arlington, Virginia, her current pride and joy is her four-legged furry baby, a pup named Coco. Laurie is a wonderful young woman and inspiration to everyone. Her cancer still is in remission today.

Laurie shared the following tips for others: "Keep your chin up. You can do it with a lot of perseverance, hard work, and a good attitude."

Laurie appreciates the following quote from Frank Lloyd Wright: "The thing always happens that you really believe in; and the belief in a thing makes it happen."

JONATHAN LANGSAM

Jonathan Langsam loves to teach learning disabled students and teachers of LD students. He and his brother Fred, who also has a learning disability and is a Wesleyan graduate, are special education teachers in the Montgomery County, Maryland, Public School system. Jonathan has not only learned to cope with dyslexia, but has helped many students learn to accept and cope with their disabilities. He has also been influential in helping other special education teachers work with students who have a variety of special needs.

Jonathan Langsam's Story

Jonathan has seen the world of LD teaching change. Words that weren't used in the late 70's when he was diagnosed with dyslexia are common today. At that time when he was in second grade, he was bussed to another town where the school had an LD class room. Although he said most of his experiences in school were good, he remembers some bad experiences such as students making fun of the LD group as they came to eat lunch.

He shared other bad experiences: "I had a few social tics that were quite visible. I was conscious of these when I was bussed into the self-contained classroom. In academic and school social situations, I used to wrinkle my nose frequently especially when I was focusing on something.

Some students called me rabbit. Several other incidents stick with me from kindergarten and elementary school. In Kindergarten I was asked to trace my name on a laminated card. We were supposed to erase the marker each time and retrace our names 10 times. I did not understand the directions and just kept copying over and over. I remember the teacher making a big issue about how I ruined the card. This really hurt and all I could do was cry." In second grade when he was placed in the self-contained class room with only eight to 10 children, he began to feel there must be something wrong with him. He didn't know it was a class for learning disabled, but he recognized he was different, especially when he was bullied and teased by others in the school. In third grade he tried to join the band at his new school because he wanted to learn to play trumpet. After two weeks he gave up since he could not learn to read music. This was another failure. All of these incidences were part of his recognition stage, leading eventually to an acceptance of his LD.

The special self-contained classroom must have been the right place for Jonathan. He stayed with the same teacher from second through sixth grade. Since the teacher accepted him, he was able to accept himself and did well academically, as well as being a leader in the class. When it was time for middle school, he began to be fearful. He still remembers his worry about leaving his teacher whom he enjoyed, and the fear of a strange school.

In some ways it was good to be back in his hometown to attend middle school, but immediately he began to feel incapable of doing the work. He was mainstreamed, and the ridicule was horrible—especially the ridicule in his own head as he felt so different. He was completely lost academically. His first report card was all D's and F's. He had gone from doing well academically to failing and didn't understand why.

Although he was starting to get more comfortable socially, he still had no idea about how to get help in the classroom. He did appreciate the experiences in the LD resource room. There he was able to get homework done early without the stress and anxiety which he would have had after school at home. His junior high experiences led to a more social life than academic one.

Jonathan feels one of the big factors that got him through elementary and junior high was the support and help from his mother. She was a teacher who worked with kids who had emotional, academic, and many other problems. Jonathan says, "She was great in helping me structure a sentence or helping me when I would "melt down" because I couldn't do a math problem. She was always there with the support I needed."

He remembers a very positive experience in junior high when he had to write a poem. He worried about stanzas and rhymes, but when he reflected on an experience in Israel, his fears were gone. His topic was, "Climbing Masada Mountain." He based it on the experience he had the previous year when he was given a trip to Israel as a Bar Mitzvah present. He was able to share the poem with feeling. The teacher praised him and his class mates also enjoyed it. He remembers feeling great and proud!

His grandfather's Bar Mitzvah present (the trip to Israel) had a tremendous effect on his life. Jonathan said that it was really his first spiritual experience and his eyes were opened to the spiritual and historical elements of his religion. One of the most memorable experiences was an event that took place at the Wailing Wall. It seemed to him the whole country was there ready to welcome a Jewish rabbi from Russia who had been locked up and persecuted for thirty or forty years and was just released. There was dancing and praying in circles. When the rabbi passed Jonathan, he reached up and touched him. Jonathan said, "The rabbi squeezed my wrist making it a spiritual experience I will never forget." In looking back, Jonathan feels that since he is a kinesthetic learner and touching is an important part of his learning, this may have helped him remember it so vividly. The entire trip to Israel was great: being at the Wailing Wall, touching the rabbi, climbing, and seeing so much of his heritage, made this his greatest learning experience in Junior High.

Because of his mother's help and his Israel experience, going to high school was not as traumatic as junior high. He enjoyed history and social studies. His self-esteem which had suffered greatly in middle school improved, and he loved the social aspects of high school—in fact, social life was much more important to him than academics at that time.

His best experience in high school occurred during his senior year. He spent nine weeks in Israel, spending most of the time in the Jerusalem area studying 4,000 years of Jewish History. This was accomplished by beginning each day at 5:00 in the morning, then riding a bus for three hours to a place which became his class room for the day. It was experiential learning, and the students role-played and lived the history. The next day there were reflective activities and he became excited about learning. He said, "This is a time in my life where I was driven by feelings and emotion. I was discovering my own heritage and learning how to learn. I learned how to challenge opinions and put thoughts on paper that make sense. My teacher was inspiring and very flamboyant. I realized I was learning about things that happened right there. This experience really helped my learning and understanding. I knew the teacher was more interested in how we experienced something than in how much work we could produce. He challenged us individually. He challenged me to read *Night* by Elie Wiesel. For the first time in my life I read a book, cover to cover! Then I wrote a four or five page paper on it. I was really proud of my accomplishment. It opened my eyes to two things: first, really learning and doing well is hard for me, and second, I can do it. It was a powerful experience for me because I learned a little about myself as a learner and gained the confidence that I could make it in college."

Until this experience, Jonathan disliked school, but his time in Israel planted seeds that opened the door to his future teaching, even though he didn't realize it then. The journal he kept is special to him today. He said, "Being independent in a foreign land taught me to problem solve, reach out for help, understand social situations better, and learn about myself. One of the best experiences was when we were on a long weekend break and decided to go to Dahab, Egypt. We had to arrange travel, money, and figure out what we were doing. For me, it is the experiences I have, coupled with my emotions and feelings, that help me learn. If I am sitting alone and reading, I am only retaining about half of the content."

Jonathan was very fortunate in junior high and high school because teachers accepted the students who went to the LD resource rooms, and they did not stand out. He felt the down side of this was that he didn't understand his disability, his learning style, and why he had some problems learning. He didn't even understand what an Individual Educational Plan (IEP) was until he was ready for college. However, he did have one teacher his senior year who made him understand that learning is a process and he had to be part of the process. This teacher's influence was important. Since Jonathan was quiet in class and didn't raise his hand to answer questions, he always gravitated to the class "clowney" stuff, and got attention by being "jokey" and silly. He now knows he needed to understand about his learning style and his strengths and weaknesses.

Today Jonathan helps his students understand these things about themselves. He told me, "In working with students with emotional disabilities, I am always trying to help teachers. One point I try to hammer home is the process of learning. Teachers are trying to make students do things rather than have them experience things within a process. As a teacher, I like to think that I meet a student on a certain letter in the alphabet. A-Z is the learning process and its content. If I meet a kid who is at D, I can't skip E, F, and G. I need to walk a student through the process, and if I get him to Z, great. If I don't, that is okay, too." His advice to teachers is, "Work with the students where they are and the rest will come."

College was a good experience for Jonathan. He said, "I remember sitting down with you and my mom in the interview process and feeling I was coming to a place where people understood my problem and I could learn. I discovered that I was right. The Learning Center was a place where I could go and feel everyone else was in the same boat and no one made a big deal about it. I was introduced to computers and new technology which helped me in my classes. I appreciated taking my exams in the Learning Center. By the end of my freshman year I knew where the support was that I needed and I was able to do college"

During college, Jonathan was more interested in social activities, especially his fraternity. He attended classes, used the Learning Center service when he felt he needed it, but he didn't go out of his way for extra help. He told me he appreciated my teaching him to understand his learning disability and learning style, advising him for classes, and placing him with professors who were flexible and willing to help students with learning disabilities. He particularly appreciated two professors who gave him oral exams, as he could do better talking than writing. In reflecting on his college experiences, he feels he gained much by four years of independent living. It was during this period he moved from recognizing his learning disability to accepting it. When one accepts his disability, he can accomplish almost anything he desires.

Probably his best experience in college occurred between his junior and senior year when he had an independent study, "Jewish Life Styles," and spent the summer at Hebrew University of Jerusalem. He spent much time in the library and also interviewed American Jews living in Israel. He asked them about their culture and spirituality, discovering what drew them to Israel. He contrasted that with his own life as a conservative Jew in America. Interviewing, collecting data and other information, resulted in a thirty page paper. He said, "This was the first time in my life that I had a topic and a deadline, but the rest was up to me." The summer proved to be a great learning experience. He said, "Here I was, a young adult in a land that was not foreign. Each day was full of possibilities and independence. Interestingly enough, this experience is highlighted by my independent endeavors to eat good food every day. I lived in a dormitory with other college students from around the world. We had a kitchen and a common area with places to sit, study, and socialize. Something inside of me made me go to the shook (open air market) and buy meat and vegetables to cook. This started a routine where I was cooking and befriending everyone in the dorm. Everybody wanted to join in and it was awesome. I had never put food/romance/adventure together in the same bowl. To make a long story short, I am now the head chef in my house, and my family can't get enough. Cooking has become an experience that I love and that my family loves too."

After returning to America, Jonathan's senior year went by quickly, and it was time to work in the "real world." He had a major in history, which he enjoyed, and a minor in education, which he had taken not because he was interested in teaching, but because he felt his mother, a special education teacher, could help him. She was especially helpful when he graduated as she recommended he consider a job as a teaching assistant in a special education class. Since the only requirement was a college degree and he had courses in education from Wesleyan, he decided to take a position as an aide in a special education school, The Resort Institute for Children and Adolescents. He worked with high school students who had emotional disabilities. This was also his mother's field.

Jonathan told me, "My first two years out of college I was a para-educator with students with emotional disabilities. What I learned in those two years is that I was still quite immature and needed a lot of work as a professional. I was also filled with a sense of how we were changing the world." He loved and was loved by the high school students. He helped them learn to read and encouraged them to attend class even when they balked at going to classes. During this time he began thinking, "Maybe I should be a teacher." After two years when his job was being phased out, it was decision time. He enjoyed the students and helping them, but there was a world with other opportunities also. His brother, Fred, managed a restaurant and he could work there or find another field.

After thinking about this, he decided to get a Master's in Special Education at Trinity College. His parents were very supportive of this decision and helped him financially so that he could be a full time student. He enjoyed his classes and, during the summer, his work in special educational programs.

After getting his Master's degree in 1997, Jonathan began working in private schools and hospital settings with students who had emotional disabilities. In 1999 he was offered a job at the Frost Center, a private school. There he was introduced to a concept called Therapeutic Community Approach. He worked there seven or eight years. He said the experience taught him the skill set, the language set, and how to work with explosive kids. Through this approach he tried to understand pain, punishment, and coercion and how they affect kids. He needed to help them take ownership for what they were doing. "This can't be done by lecturing", Jonathan said. He also stated, "What I have experienced and learned throughout the last 15 years in this field is that the best tool in helping others lies within our abilities to help ourselves and the communities around us. I am lucky that I get to be part of an exciting job: helping students achieve their goals. One of the biggest challenges comes when a student is not achieving and we need to find out within ourselves as to why. Most of the answers are right there in front of us."

In 2005 Jonathan moved from the private to the public education system. Approaches he learned in the private sector have helped him to teach others. He and his brother, Fred, travel to other schools and work with teachers who are working with emotionally disturbed kids. He is using an approach called Circle of Courage. (See Web site, Circle of Courage.) This approach has roots in the Native American Culture of child rearing. Jonathan uses four components: belonging, independence, mastery, and generosity, to guide teachers in their teaching. In addition to teaching teachers he is also teaching disabled students following this method. His students have both learning and emotional disabilities to overcome. Jonathan finds his work challenging and enjoyable. He has fun reaching many people and touching their lives. Jonathan is not only a good teacher, but he is a good husband and good father of two children.

Jonathan's Tips for LD Young People:

1. Know your learning style, how you learn as a learner, and how to use this knowledge.
2. Don't be afraid to get help.

Note: Some of Jonathan's tips for teachers are in the chapter in this book: "Tips for Teachers."

JENNIFER SHAW FOSKO

Jennifer Fosko is very dedicated and service oriented, working hard to help others. She is a 1994 graduate of West Virginia Wesleyan College, where she majored in psychology, which has opened many career opportunities. She has worked with children, youth and adults. Her future plans are to become a certified special education teacher. She and her husband, Kevin, are parents of Bobby, a wonderful son whom they adopted from Guatemala. Jennifer has learned to cope with her learning disability and hopes her story will be helpful to others.

Jennifer's Story

Jennifer remembers struggling in elementary school and wanting so much to succeed. She attended a fine Catholic School, but at a time when little was known about learning disabilities. Jennifer now knows her disabilities were in processing and memorization, which caused problems for her in reading and math. As a result she had some painful experiences. She remembers some of her peers calling her stupid and a retard. Often she would get papers back with a large F in red and also comments in red. At other times the red F's were simply circled, but many of her classmates saw them and snickered. One teacher pulled her ears and pecked her on the head. This teacher kept calling her, "Jenny," which was a name she disliked.

In eighth grade she had a teacher who did not understand what Jennifer meant when she kept telling her she had a learning disability. The teacher couldn't understand Jennifer's difficulties. Finally Jennifer's mother came to the school and tried to explain Jennifer's problems and why the class was so difficult for her. Jennifer remembers her mother crying when she tried to make the teacher understand. She says her mother was her best advocate. She was "a stay at home Mom" who devoted a great deal of time to her children, especially Jennifer who had special needs. She helped Jennifer with homework and also gave her emotional support.

Jennifer calls her mother, "her rock." Jennifer's two younger sisters were also supportive. They helped fight her battles when other children teased her. Later when she was in college, they would call and say, "You can do it! You can do it!" Their support still means much to her.

Jennifer not only remembers her eighth grade problems, but also a wonderful teacher, Mrs. Daly. Jennifer said she was incredible. When Jennifer was upset she would sit with her and together they would work through Jennifer's problems. Mrs. Daly helped Jennifer prepare for high school by teaching her how to deal with difficult teachers. She understood Jennifer's needs and fears. She was able to encourage Jennifer to believe she could succeed in high school.

Although Jennifer struggled at times, she did succeed in high school. The school had a learning center and the teachers in the center were wonderful. They taught her study skills which she found helpful in high school and in college. A counselor shared with her a list of colleges that had majors that interested Jennifer. She was encouraged in her junior year to visit several schools including Wesleyan. She said that after her interview and tour at Wesleyan, she had a warm feeling and told her mother, "I loved this school."

Her initial feeling was correct. Wesleyan provided a quality education in a warm atmosphere. The first month of school was difficult. Classes were much harder and there was much more reading than in high school. To make matters worse she was very homesick. Jennifer said she appreciated Shawn Kuba, the learning center counselor, because both Shawn and I spent time allowing her to cry and share her fears and unhappiness. She said to me, "Shawn and you were my shinning lights."

Jennifer gradually got over her homesickness, but another hurdle was taking exams. She had great test anxiety. She said she would always remember Judy Knorr, the testing supervisor, who took time with Jennifer before she would begin an exam, encouraging her and helping to reduce her test anxiety. Judy was always positive when she handed her the test, reassuring her that she would do well. This seemed to make taking a test less overwhelming.

By the end of the semester Jennifer had adjusted to college. She had made many friends and was enjoying college life. She told me that she is glad she took both developmental math and developmental writing her freshman year. They gave her the foundation for upper level courses. She appreciated many of her classes. Dr. William Mahoney made history come alive, and Katherine Glenney, one of her psychology professors, was always there for her with help and encouragement.

Even after her successful freshman year, college was not always easy for Jennifer. There were difficult classes and times of stress. During the first semester of her senior year, she had a "down time." She even felt she wanted to drop out of college, but her roommate, Dawn Mitchell, and a good friend, Stephanie Fairbanks, were able to help her. She said basically they gave her advice on how to do assignments, telling her to take small steps at a time, and not try to do the whole assignment at once. She needed them and this type of support to help her manage stress and not be overwhelmed. Realizing how important their support was to her, Jennifer has helped others in similar ways.

After graduation, Jennifer knew she wanted to make a positive difference in other people's lives. She felt her psychology major gave her background to fulfill this goal. She began working as an activities assistant at Bedford Court in Silver Spring, MD. This was a senior living facility with three different levels of care: independent living, assisted living, and skilled nursing activities. Jennifer helped to provide various activities on a daily basis for the residents and they responded very appreciatively. Not everything was pleasant, however. Jennifer thought that coping with remarks about her disability would be in the past when she finished her education. She was wrong! She had a boss at work that discovered Jennifer had a learning disability. She treated Jennifer differently and degraded her. Jennifer said she was able to ignore this and not allow it to hurt her. As a result, she said it made her stronger because of the help from a co-worker who is one of her really good friends today. After five years, Jennifer began feeling burned out and decided to work at the other end of the age spectrum, with children.

Jennifer began working in 2001 at Capital City Public Charter School in Washington, DC. At the end of the school year, she married Kevin Fosko. They moved to Pennsylvania where she worked at Hillside School, a school for children with learning disabilities. She enjoyed being an aid in the kindergarten classroom where she had the opportunity to teach young children the alphabet, beginning math, and other types of learning activities. She loved the children.

Although she thoroughly enjoyed her work, she felt it was time to think of being certified to teach, and began taking classes at Cedar Cress College. After a year in Pennsylvania, she was homesick and she and Kevin decided to move back to Maryland. There she took a position as a teacher assistant at The National Center for Children and Families, which is a nonprofit organization in Bethesda, MD. One of their goals was to enable teenagers to transition into a mainstream high school. She worked hard teaching troubled teens and knows she was reaching many. However, she was nearly assaulted by one of the teenagers, which was a terrible experience for her. After a year she transferred to the homeless shelter on the same campus in order to work with children.

In 2005 Jennifer began working at the Gymboree Play and Music Center in Silver Spring, Maryland. She began as a teacher. Jennifer taught classes for parents, helping their children reach different developmental milestones. Later she was promoted and became site manager where she ran the site, supervised and trained staff while continuing to teach. She was again promoted and became marketing coordinator. In this capacity she went to different businesses to promote the center. She also gave introductory classes to mom's groups, teaching those who had just given birth.

In 2007 while Jennifer was working at the Gymboree Play and Music Center, she and Kevin adopted their son, Bobby, from Guatemala. They had waited patiently for fifteen months while all the paper work was completed. Waiting was often frustrating. Jennifer believes this was too long a period.

Bobby is now in elementary school at St Francis International School where his dad, Kevin, is technology and testing coordinator. Jennifer worked also as a "floating" instructional assistant, working with two to four year olds there. Because of knee surgery she had to resign since she couldn't get down on the floor with little children. Bobby enjoys classes. He is especially interested in his Indian heritage. He asked his mother if there were any Indians left. She answered, "YOU." When Bobby is older and would like to learn more about his heritage, the Foskos plan to travel with Bobby so he can visit some Indian reservations and learn more about Indians, especially the Mayan culture.

Since adopting Bobby, Jennifer has spent lots of time being a mother, enjoying and watching Bobby develop into a fine boy. She has spent time at home and also has worked both part time and full time teaching children. Much of her time has been spent pursuing a Post-baccalaureate Certification in special education. She has done so well that she currently has a GPA of 3.75 with only has one class left to take. She has been very happy with her studies and fine professors. Before beginning this Certification program she had taken other graduate courses always making A's and B's.

Jennifer has had some major problems. Her test anxiety, learning disability, and eye problems have created hurdles for her in trying to pass the reading and math portions of the Praxis 1, a test needed for teacher certification. She will be studying and taking the Praxis II Special Education Content and Knowledge Area test for the first time. Jennifer is in the process of working with an Educational Psychologist to update her documentation so that she can get the necessary accommodations. Meanwhile she has accepted a position as a part-time Special Education Teacher at the Mother of God School in Gaithersburg, MD.

When Jennifer passes the tests, she will be eligible to complete the Accelerated Post-baccalaureate Special Education Certification Program. She also hopes to start taking classes towards her Masters of Education in Special Education. Jennifer's life journey has not been easy but her dedication to others and her determination to succeed, have allowed her to be successful.

Jennifer hopes the following tips will be helpful for others:

1. Never give up.
2. Do your best.
3. Don't be afraid to ask for help.
4. Believe that you can do anything you are determined to do.
5. Get appropriate accommodations for taking tests.
6. While in college use the accommodations you need.

AMY SHEARMAN O'BRIEN

Amy Shearman O'Brien and Drs. Herb and Phyllis Coston

Amy is a person who understands learning disabilities from many points of view. She is a mother of four learning disabled children; she has taught LD classes in a public school; she has experienced what it is like to be a student with a learning disability. Amy has perceptual impairment which includes dyscalculia (problems with math), dysgraphia (problems with writing), fine motor problems, hand-eye coordination and visual coordination. She has had to develop coping strategies to succeed.

Amy's Story

These problems caused great anxiety in school. The most painful experience was not knowing why she was having so much trouble, as the work seemed to come easily to others in her class. Her teachers would remark, "She is such a sweet child." However, they were unable to give advice or suggest ways to help her. To make matters worse, she was told by her classmates that she was stupid. They often made fun of her. Amy's mother was her advocate and supported her. She helped her develop a good self-concept by working with her and telling the teachers that her daughter was not stupid.

She remembers second grade as a painful time. Because she had such problems in math she was told to go to a teacher for special help twice a week. When she got up to leave the room, her teacher said to her, "Sit down; you don't need that." In front of the whole class she was made to feel like a fool and felt everyone probably thought she was. She just sat there feeling horrible but continued trying to do the math work sheets without receiving any support. It wasn't until 4th grade she began to receive help.

There were other learning issues in junior high school. She remembers how hard she studied for a test on Macbeth. She felt she knew it, but her anxiety level was so high that she couldn't remember the material, and she flunked the test. Despite her family's support and the help of tutors, junior high and high school were not pleasant experiences. She shudders when she remembers walking to her Special Ed classes and hearing other students say, "That's where all the 'slow' people go." The only place she felt safe was on the track team where she found nothing but encouragement and no criticism. Track was the bright star in her high school experience. She said, "Running track was the only place I felt important and safe from criticism." She was a good runner and her coaches were amazingly supportive.

It was during her senior year that she found a pamphlet about West Virginia Wesleyan and the support they offered for students with learning disabilities. She said, "After a positive interview with Mrs. Coston, I knew I had found a place where I would feel valued and welcomed." This was a relief, as during the formative years her family members were her strongest supporters and her only advocates. She made it through high school and came to Wesleyan on a partial athletic scholarship for cross country and track.

Due to a few caring teachers, Amy felt that one day she would like to be a teacher and help students similar to her—students feeling completely lost and overwhelmed. She realized that she was extremely lucky to have a supportive family as many students do not. She wanted to be able to help such students one day. A major in education would help her fulfill this dream, and Wesleyan had an excellent Education Department.

When Amy arrived at Wesleyan, she felt comfortable. When she asked professors if she could take her tests in the Learning Center, they acted like it was no big deal, and her tests were ready for her when she arrived at the center. The Learning Center staff was friendly and helpful, never making her feel she was out of place when she went there for help. This reinforced her idea of wanting to teach so she could help other students realize it was okay to receive help.

While a student at Wesleyan, Amy became a cross country and track star. She also became a student assistant in the Learning Center and a staff member in the summer program for high school juniors with learning disabilities. She was helpful and loved by the students. Several talked with her about becoming teachers and they did fulfill their dreams. * This also reinforced her desire to teach. She was beginning to help others realize that while things will be more difficult, you can succeed and have a career and family if you choose.

Amy did become a teacher and helped students at the middle school level. After the birth of her premature twins she was no longer able to work outside the home. As her family grew, she realized that each of their children had some type of learning disability. Amy believes her own experiences and her education have allowed her to be able to help them accept their disabilities and realize that they are gifted, although they may learn differently from others. She has told them that if you fail it is okay, as long as you know in your heart you have done your best. She also shares with them what her mother told her, "Not everyone understands learning disabilities and as a result they misunderstand differences in the ways people learn."

Amy helps her children do their homework by encouraging them to take notes in some classes and look over them at night. She has helped them make flash cards as a way of reviewing. She has put information on a CD to help them with auditory learning. She emphasizes that patience and praise are very important!

Amy believes parents and teachers ought to share their own struggles and experiences with their children. They also should help children understand their gifts, not just their differences. As a former teacher she knows the ins and outs of the educational system and is able to advocate on a level different from many other parents. She is not intimidated by the school. Through her example, her own children and others can see what they are able to accomplish in their lives. Someday she will return to teaching in a school system, but right now she has a full-time job at home.

***See the stories about Kelly Paxton and Patricia Boothe.
**Some of Amy's ideas and tips are in the chapters, "Tips for Teachers", and "Tips for parents."

1990 Wesleyan Woman's Track Team

KATHERINE KIMES

Katherine's life was dramatically changed August 1989, two days before she was to begin her junior year in high school. She was in an auto accident which resulted in a traumatic brain injury. With great determination she worked hard to overcome the physical, cognitive and psychosocial consequences of the injury. She is a successful adult today.

Katherine Kimes' Story

When Katherine was 16 years old she was a passenger in the front seat of a car that went out of control hitting a mail box, breaking a telephone pole in half, and hitting a tree. Although she had her seat belt on, she still received a major brain injury. Her brain stem was twisted and stretched; she immediately went into a coma and had a post traumatic seizure at the scene of the accident. She was life-flighted immediately to Allegheny Hospital in Pittsburgh, Pa.

Katherine remained in a coma for four weeks. Upon regaining consciousness she could not walk; her tongue was paralyzed and she could not talk nor eat; the left side was severely impaired and her cognitive skills were greatly compromised. After slowly regaining consciousness from the coma she began rehabilitation. She spent several months at the rehabilitation center until the insurance ran out. Her parents, knowing it was important, continued to pay for the rehab. Doctors told her parents that it was highly unlikely she would graduate from high school without major assistance and higher education was out of the question. Katherine and her parents were unwilling to accept this analysis. Twenty-two years later Katherine has a BA, two Master's Degrees, and a Doctor's degree in Special Education.

Accomplishing this has not been easy, but Katherine has been determined and motivated. After many rehab sessions and much persistence she was able to return to Richland High School in Gibsonia, Pa, for the second semester of her junior year. Although she had been an honor student, she wasn't able to return to regular classes, but was placed in two LD classes and demoted to the lower level education classes. Through hard work and determination, she was able not only to graduate on time from high school in 1991, but also graduated in the top 10% of her class.

During Katherine's senior year she applied to Wesleyan because of our Special Service Program. After her interviews, Director of Admissions, Bob Skinner, and I wanted to give her the opportunity to attend Wesleyan. We did not have any traumatic brain injured students at that time. I had worked with one traumatic brain injured student, Andy Irons, before the Special Service Program was in place. At that time, I had no training in how to work with brain injuries but I used my instincts and knowledge of teaching reading to help Andy achieve. I knew if we were going to be successful with Katherine, I needed a staff member who was willing to receive specialized training and spend a lot of time with her. I chose Alice Dillon who was a young mother with preschool children. I had observed her patience and caring attitude with her children, and students with whom she worked always gave me glowing reports. Alice was the right choice. During the summer, she and I attended a conference at the University of Connecticut concerning working with students who have experienced traumatic brain injuries. The conference was very helpful. Alice continued studying about brain injuries and spent hours working with Katherine. They had a wonderful relationship and Katherine was successful.

Katherine's major was Sociology, and the late Dr. John Warner helped her tremendously. John was chairman of the Sociology department, a minister, and a wonderful caring professor. Each student was important to him. He and Alice Dillon worked well together helping Katherine. In addition to her Sociology major, she minored in English. Writing was Alice's specialty in the Learning Center. She had a special way of encouraging students, which was helpful to Katherine. Alice recalls that upon her entrance to college, Katherine was still working on regaining the language skills that had been compromised by the brain injury. Often times when they reviewed essays and papers that she had written for her classes, Katherine was frustrated because certain sentences were not conveying precisely what she intended. She was not content to let that go even if the sentences were grammatically correct; but neither was she looking for somebody to revise her papers for her. Struggling with word and language recall, Katherine was painstaking about her own revisions and utilized Alice as a sounding board for her ideas and written work. Alice believes that the persistence Katherine demonstrated in her writing mirrored her overall motivation to achieve her goals despite the significant injury that she sustained. Dr. Warner and Alice encouraged her and helped her be successful in her pursuit of higher education. She graduated from Wesleyan in 1995.

Katherine's educational experiences did not end with her BA Degree from Wesleyan. She pursued a Master's Degree in Professional Technical and Literary Writing, graduating from De Paul University in May of 2000. Later she received a second Master's Degree from George Washington University in 2004 from the School of Education and Human Development. This MA was in Transitional Special Education with an emphasis in Acquired Brain Injury.

In August 2009 Katherine received a doctor's degree in Special Education from George Washington University with an emphasis in brain injury. She was part of the Leaders for System Change Project.

While pursuing her doctorate at George Washington University, her advisor was Carol Kochhar-Bryant, Senior Associate Dean, Department of Teacher Preparation and Special Education of the Graduate School of Education and Human Development. Katherine said she made a big impact on her life.

There are two issues which Katherine feels need improvement in our society: school systems and teachers more able to teach brain injured students effectively, and employers more willing to hire brain injured workers.

Katherine shared that employment is a big issue for her and for other physically challenged persons. She and others have the education and the ability, but finding someone to hire them is a big problem. Katherine currently works for United Cerebral Palsy/Community Living and Support Services. She feels one of the reasons she was hired by this company is that the CEO of the company, Al Condeluci, is a well-known person in the disability field. He has published books in the field, and believes hiring persons with disabilities is important.

In Katherine's present position she coordinates services and support for persons with disabilities so they can live independently within the community. As part of her work she visits these persons and assesses their needs at home. She enjoys her work. In the future she hopes to develop her career further and work more directly within the field of brain injury. She would enjoy teaching or doing research at a university in the area of special education and brain injury.

Katherine's dissertation, finished in 2009, dealt with a case study of one school district's efforts to work with students who had traumatic brain injury, to help them learn more effectively. Literally millions of Americans live with the effects of a long term brain injury. The need to improve education for brain injured students and veterans are a challenge about which Katherine feels deeply.

New Directions, Spring 2009, (a publication of George Washington University) contains an article, "Extraordinary Courage," which quotes Katherine: "Unfortunately, brain injury has slipped under our educators' radar . . . It has often gone unnoticed due to underreporting and/or misidentification . . . Important steps need to be taken in order to change our educational system across the nation if we are to meet the challenge of educating students with brain injuries." Katherine would hope to be a part of making these changes.

Katherine has been featured in at least five print releases and has written over 15 articles for journals and newsletters. She has also given presentations at the North Dakota Department of Public Instruction, the Council of Exceptional Children, George Washington University, The North American Brain Injury Society, and State Conference of the Brain Injury Society of South Carolina. Katherine is a remarkable women and an inspiration to many!

Katherine's Tip:

>Never give up!

MARK DANGORA

Mark is a cancer survivor, an educator, a loving father and husband. He is a man of courage and determination whose story is truly inspirational!

Mark's Story

Mark is the Assistant Principal of Rochester Middle School, in Rochester, New Hampshire. One of the reasons he is well liked by students and staff is that he understands the students and their problems. While growing up he experienced similar problems in school. He was often sent to the principal's office because of his mischievous behavior. He hated parent-teacher nights, and remembers one time hiding under his bed so he wouldn't have to face his parents when they returned home. It didn't work. His father confronted him and it was not a pleasant experience! Mark is amused now at the irony of his present job, dealing with students who are sent to his office.

Mark's parents and siblings were very successful. Mark was the youngest of five children. His parents did not understand why he was different from their other children and did not live up to their expectations. His problems began in kindergarten. He said that he felt sick in his stomach and knew instinctively that he would not do well in school. His first grade teacher would walk around the classroom and would berate him and his work if he performed poorly. She would stop at his desk and slap it with the yard stick because she was not pleased with his work. He always felt like crying, his stomach was constantly upset, and his school experience was miserable.

Mark's most demoralizing experience occurred in third grade. He was not promoted with the rest of his class. His honesty with his teacher had not helped him. Since his homework was better than his class work, the teacher asked him if it was his work. He said, "No, my Dad did it." This may have contributed to his failure. It seemed to him that everyone called him stupid! As a result he believed it. When he did move into fourth and fifth grade, he was a hellion, disrupting the classes often. His disrupting behavior continued in middle school. He remembers thinking, "If I am stupid and can't do the work, I'll mess around and disrupt the class." He frustrated his teachers, his parents, and himself.

As a last resort, his parents sent him to a boarding school, Worcester Academy in Worcester Massachusetts. He knows it was a very good school, but every day he struggled academically. Because he had not been diagnosed with a learning disability, no one really understood him and he did not understand himself. Mark's misbehavior continued at Worcester Academy. Mark liked his roommate who was from Bangkok, Thailand. However, the roommate asked to change rooms because Mark ate all of the roommate's cookies that had been sent to him from Thailand.

One of Mark's worst experiences was standing before the class to read. He was always embarrassed because the words ran together and he could simply not read them. Again he felt stupid! School continued to be a painful experience. He did enjoy athletics, especially track and cross country running. His social life was fine because he was such a handsome athletic guy. But reading was a nightmare.

His parents were concerned about his future. They expected him to go to college, but also realized that he needed a small school where he could receive support. Mark wanted to go to college and please his parents, but he had fears of failure. His attitude changed when he met Paul Willis, a recruiter from West Virginia Wesleyan College who visited Mark's high school. Paul, who had been an outstanding athlete on Wesleyan's soccer team, was energetic and was truly concerned about students. He helped Mark feel he could succeed, and that West Virginia Wesleyan had a support program which would fit his needs. Paul encouraged Mark to apply.

After applying, Mark discovered that to be accepted in Wesleyan's support program, it was necessary to have been tested for a learning disability. Finally in twelfth grade he was tested, and it was discovered that he was smart, not stupid, and he had a learning disability, dyslexia. This was helpful for him to know and to finally understand why he had been having difficulties for so many years. He wasn't stupid after all!

Mark says one of the happiest moments, of his life, other than the marriage to his wife Karen and the birth of his two boys, Henry and Wally, was receiving the acceptance letter from Wesleyan. His joy was not unfounded because he had a good and successful college career. He especially appreciated Shawn Kuba, the learning center counselor, who helped him improve his self-esteem.

Every silver lining seems to have a cloud. A bad experience at Wesleyan occurred his first semester. He was really excited that he was able to take his tests untimed in the Learning Center Testing Lab. He had studied and knew he would do well, and was looking forward to calling his parents with good news about his grade. When he received the test and opened it, his heart fell. He read over the questions and his mind went blank! He sat there not knowing what to do. Finally he remembered he had in his pocket some questions and answers he had used in studying for the test. He carefully pulled out these study notes, looking around to make sure no one was watching him, and began to cheat. The supervisor of the testing lab saw him and immediately asked him to leave the lab and go into a room with her. He remembers the experience vividly. He said "She chewed me up and down royally and I felt very guilty and so ashamed." She reminded him it was a privilege to take the test in the lab and he had abused this opportunity. It was a traumatic experience for him. He said that he was so distraught that he cried, and said, "Please! Please forgive me!" Mark said it was a turnaround moment in his life, and he never cheated again. He told me that today when students are sent to his office for cheating, he says, "Let me tell you a story." He believes his story has helped many others.

Mark had many wonderful experiences at Wesleyan. He began to enjoy learning and was able to have success. He appreciated his history classes and became a history major. Since he enjoyed history and Wesleyan encouraged travel abroad, he participated in a semester at sea sponsored by the University of Pittsburgh. During this four month period he visited 20 different countries, one of which was South Africa. There he had the opportunity to meet Bishop Tutu in Capetown, South Africa. An additional overseas opportunity for Mark was taking a Wesleyan January Term class in Bulgaria with other Wesleyan students.

One of the most important ways that Wesleyan helped Mark was to inspire him to help "change the world." He became an activist, participating in opportunities to help others and to protect and improve the environment. In 1993 Mark co-founded the recycling program on the campus of West Virginia Wesleyan College. This program is still flourishing at Wesleyan. He also participated in a program to help clean the Little Kanawha River. During a spring break he drove to Salisbury, Maryland, to help build a house for Habitat for Humanity. By his senior year, he began thinking of ways he could be a useful citizen and make a difference in the world. He dreamed about joining the Peace Corp or AmeriCorps.

After graduation he worked as an aide to the mayor of Leominster, Massachusetts. In this position he managed a recycling program for this city of 35,000 people. In addition he wrote grants and handled various constituent complaints. He enjoyed the work, but knew he wanted to do something else to serve others.

The opportunity came in 1996 when he joined the AmeriCorps, fulfilling one of his dreams. He was sent to Lyons, Georgia where he worked with the Toombs County AmeriCorps program as a member of a team and as a third grade teacher. In this role, he not only taught elementary students, but also mentored 12 children of migrant workers in an after school program. He loved the kids and they loved him. He was appreciated by his colleagues also. One teacher wrote, "Mr. Dangora has the rare gift of putting himself in the other person's shoes." The AmeriCorps program was a great experience. As a result, he knew he wanted to teach even though he had not taken education courses in college.

After fulfilling his commitment to AmeriCorps, Mark began work as a paraprofessional at Rupert Nook Middle School in Newburyport, MA. Here he aided in the instruction of World History to seventh graders; tutored 6 seventh grade learning disabled students individually in basic grammar; and assisted students with autism and other special needs on a one-on-one basis.

In 1998 Mark had another opportunity to work in the AmeriCorps program. He joined the Youth Star AmeriCorps program in Chelsea, Massachusetts. In this position he mentored AmeriCorps members; instructed classes in GED; taught college preparatory classes; and implemented curriculum.

When his term with AmeriCorps was over in 2001, he wanted to fulfill another dream. He applied and was accepted into the Peace Corp to serve in Lesotho, Africa. However, 9/11 came and Peace Corp opportunities were on hold for six months. He had to take a job while waiting. An interesting opportunity was offered. He was hired as an adjunct professor at Boricua College, a multicultural school in Brooklyn, New York. Mark found himself as the youngest professor and the only Caucasian faculty member. He made many friends with the students and other faculty members. He taught in both the History and Education Departments. It was a great experience.

During this six month period while waiting for the Peace Corp program to resume, he became reacquainted with Karen Williams. When they were both children their families vacationed in New Hampshire and they became friends. Now 10 or 15 years later they began dating. He knew this was the girl he wanted to marry and he did not accept the Peace Corp assignment when it came.

They were married in 2004. A year later their first son, Henry, was born and in 2007 another son, Wally, joined the family. They were so happy to have two sons, but were saddened to learn that Wally was born deaf. Having a handicapped child is both a problem and a challenge. They knew that they would accept this opportunity to do everything to help him grow up as normally as possible. They began by learning sign language and reading and studying about the deaf community. As Wally grew, his hearing improved. This occurs in only 1% if the cases. It was wonderful news! Both Karen and Mark are so pleased and feel blessed to have two wonderful children. They both enjoy doing activities with their sons. Mark has coached Henry's kindergarten soccer, basketball, and baseball teams.

Mark loved his teaching experiences but as a married man he knew he must be qualified to teach in the public as well as the private systems. He attended Curry College in 2005, graduating with a Master's Degree in Education. Curry was a good school to attend. Professors understood students with Learning Disabilities although no assistance was given to graduate students. Before the Americans With Disabilities Act, Curry had a program supporting students with learning disabilities, similar to Wesleyan's.

In 2005, they moved to New Hampshire, and he began teaching World History at Alvine High School in Hudson, New Hampshire and Karen taught middle school science in Stratham, New Hampshire. In addition to teaching, Mark served on the New Hampshire Department of Education School and Improvement Team. Mark taught at Alvine for three years and then became Assistant Principal at Parkside Middle School in Manchester, New Hampshire.

An administrator's life at a middle school is extremely busy and challenging. Mark assisted the principal in observing, evaluating, and supporting 125 teachers and paraprofessionals. He had numerous projects. As assistant principal he handled discipline problems. His own middle school experiences of spending a great deal of time in the principal's office for misbehavior gave him insight and understanding in handling problems. Mark thrived on a busy schedule and many challenges. He was pleased with his life and opportunities for service.

Suddenly everything changed for Mark! He will never forget Wally's first birthday. A small family party was planned and during a break in his work he thought of plans for this special birthday. His thoughts were interrupted by a phone call. It was a call that would change his life, and one he would never forget. The voice on the other end identified himself as Mark's doctor. He had the results of tests that Mark had taken, and because there was a problem suggested Mark come to the office very soon. Mark said, "Tell me what is wrong **now**!" After a short pause which seemed like an eternity the doctor said, "Mark, you have cancer." "No," Mark said, "You must be mistaken." The doctor explained that there was no mistake. Mark had throat cancer. Mark insisted that throat cancer was for "old men" and he was only in his thirties. A trip to the doctor's office and seeing the x-rays made him realize it was true and he accepted the diagnosis. There was no mistake!

After the diagnosis the treatments began and Mark became very sick. The cancer was growing and his prognosis was not good. He had to leave his job, but the school district said they would keep it for him and encouraged him to get better. He appreciated their support, but he became worse and was hospitalized. He and others believed he was losing ground and was on his death bed. At this time he began praying and meditating. His mind went back to Wesleyan days, and he pictured a place, The Pringle Tree, which was a small park off campus where he would go to think. Now this image was helping him.

The Pringle Tree is an historical place in Upshur County, West Virginia. It is the place where the Pringle brothers who were deserters in the French and Indian War fled from Fort Pitt and found refuge in a large tree which was hollowed out making a small room. They remained there until they ran out of ammunition for hunting, sought out civilization, and learned the war was over. The tree which Mark had experienced was the third generation of that tree on the bank of the Buckhannon River. Mark had enjoyed telling his children the story about it.

Prayer and meditation were important to Mark. He felt he had much to live for: a wonderful family and a job which allowed him to make a difference in the lives of others. As his cancer got worse, he was transferred to a hospital that was farther away from his home, and he could not see his children. In order to continue a relationship with his children, he began writing children's stories. His stories were about two dogs that he called Riff and Ruff. On good days he was able to write the stories. His children loved them. This proved to be good therapy for Mark. (One of his stories, *Riff and Ruff go to the Exeter Train Station*, and an entry from the journal he kept in the hospital, are printed at the end of this chapter.)

Mark battled with cancer for two years. He lost over 50 pounds and went through periods when he didn't expect to live. He says he went through Hell and back. The recovery was a long, slow, grueling process and he still feels dull pains of cancer both emotionally and physically.

Today Mark is an Assistant Principal of Rochester Middle School which is in one of the largest school districts in New Hampshire. He has many responsibilities and is grateful to be alive and working. He is also working on a doctoral program at the University of New Hampshire.

I was privileged to see many recommendations about Mark. I'd like to close this chapter with a quote from one of the Language Arts teachers who worked under him. She wrote, "One of Mark's finest qualities is his infectious enthusiasm, and it spills over onto the teachers, which essentially works its way into the hearts of the students. His positive outlook made Mark approachable, easy to ask advice from, and most importantly, as a teacher I feel supported by him as my chief administrator. The students are receptive to Mark because he treats them fairly and with respect. I have noticed that whether he is dealing with students, teachers or parents, he respects people and is genuinely interested in the well-being of others."

Mark's Expectations and Rules for success:

1. Greet people on a daily basis with a smile.
2. Don't assume and always ask questions.
3. No matter what, be respectful.
4. Do your best!
5. Always do what's best for kids, not grownups.

Riff and Ruff go to the Exeter Train Station:

One day Riff and Ruff went to the Exeter train station with their mommy and daddy. Riff and Ruff loved trains. They also loved going to the train station to watch the trains pass by. Today they waited patiently for the 12:17 PM passenger train to Portland, Maine. The first sign of the train was the loud "choo-choo" sound of the train horn and the sound of the rail road crossing "ding, dings". The train was on time and "Wooshed" into the station. The train's color was silver and purple and had five large cars on it. One car was a food car where the passengers could eat hot dogs, potato chips, sandwiches and drink soda and hot cocoa. The train conductor was dressed in black and wore a black top hat. He yelled all aboard!!

Next stop! Durham, New Hampshire! Riff and Ruff watched the train leave the station and waved goodbye. What a lovely visit to the train station, Riff and Ruff.

What a lovely day!

A short story that has helped me throughout my education years:

I have an old friend who was a farmer in New England that gave me some valuable advice. I call it the "cow patty story":

He had cows on his farm. The cow poop/patties always had to be cleaned up on the farm. The old farmer would wait a day or two for the patties to harden to make it easier to be picked up. A fresh soft patty always made a mess, smelled awful and was very difficult to manage.

He used this theory and applied to interacting with people. He told me when tempers flare and interactions with them get hostile you should apply the Cow Patty theory. Keep a cool head, don't overreact to the drama, and sit on your anger for a day or two. Then you can conclude the conversation with a cool and collected head. I try to use this theory on a daily basis in my work. If a parent, teacher or student is expressing loud anger or frustration, I hear them out and continue the conversation a day or two later. This way the conversation will be much easier to clean up.

JAMES HOFFMAN

Teaching is in Jim Hoffman's blood. He loves working with students both as a teacher and an administrator. Jim is one of many learning disabled students who become teachers so they can give the next generation of LD students the help they need in school. Jim graduated from West Virginia Wesleyan College in 1995 as an Education major with a concentration in Special Education. Most of his career as teacher and administrator has been in the Orange County

School District in Orlando, Florida, where he is presently the Assistant Principal of Lake Nona High School.

Jim's Story

From the beginning, Jim was a very active child who would not sit still to be read to, and had little interest in children's TV programs that did not contain lots of action. He became very frustrated over simple things such as a sandwich not halved into triangles and any snack cracker or cookie not being perfectly shaped. At the same time he could sit for hours playing with Lego and listening to music, especially Sousa marches. As he grew older, he became more frustrated over little things. However, he became very independent and self-reliant.

Jim attended nursery school; but he displayed no interest or excitement in learning the very basic curriculum. Several weeks into his enrollment in a private kindergarten, the director/teacher who was a former teacher of learning disabled students, informed his parents that she felt Jim was displaying indications of learning difficulties. Tests showed no obvious brain damage and Jim started speech therapy.

Soon after this, the family moved to Pittsburgh where he was enrolled in a Montessori Kindergarten. Although the Montessori schools gave Jim the freedom to pursue his interests, he could not deal with its lack of structure. The lack of classroom structure was to remain a problem for Jim throughout his public school days.

When Jim was registered and tested for entrance into public school, his mother informed the school officials what the kindergarten teacher had shared and suggested that perhaps he should be tested. No effort was made to test Jim. His first grade teachers continued to report that he was a very active child, perhaps somewhat immature but that he would "catch up" before long.

Things came to a crisis during second grade. Jim was having behavior problems and the teacher seemed unable to know what to do. It was during this period that his mother discovered that he could not read. He had brought home a reading test on which he had missed every question. When asked to read the questions, his mother was shocked to learn that he could not read the questions. At that moment Jim's mother became his advocate! She called the school and informed the principal of her discovery. She asked for an explanation from the teacher. She also informed the school that she wanted Jim to be tested and if arrangements were not made she would go to the next school board meeting and tell them of the school's neglect in testing Jim and in informing the parents of the severity of his reading problem. A call was also placed to the Director of Psychological Services. Within a week, arrangements were made and Jim was tested.

One of the results of the testing was to discover he was a kinesthetic learner. His parents knew he was very active, but hadn't used this term. His mother dropped in to observe him in class so she could understand this term better, and see how it affected him and his teachers. She shared this experience with his father who was a high school principal. Jim's father was able to work with Jim's teachers and get more testing for him, including the testing which could diagnose his learning disability.

Jim's mother felt it was important to include the previous episode in this story. She feels that because Jim's father was an administrator in the same school system, one that was/is recognized for its excellence by both the US and the Pennsylvania Department of Education, the teachers and principal felt Jim's problem would be an **embarrassment** to his parents. Instead of trying to correct the problem, they avoided it and passed it to the next person.

Jim was competing in a school district where over ninety-five percent of the graduates attended a four year college/university. In this situation he was exposed to highly motivated peers. At times this led to Jim's worry about failure and it hurt his self-esteem. This is one of the reasons his parents felt the situation should have been dealt with immediately.

When the school wasn't dealing with the problem, the parents did. Since Jim was an only child, he received lots of attention and his parents were able to provide opportunities for success outside of the classroom. Sports seemed like a good outlet to channel his energy. However, baseball was too slow, soccer was great as long as he was not standing on the sideline, and tennis was better than baseball. Running was his sport! Jim won his age division in the first 5K race he entered and from then through middle school, high school, and college, Jim received success in track and field and cross country racing. To Jim, running was wonderful.

In addition to sports, music was another outlet. He was able to pursue his interest in music through playing the trumpet in elementary, middle, and high school, as well as college. His musical ability earned him a small scholarship to West Virginia Wesleyan College.

The extra activities were great in elementary, junior high, and high school; but he felt frustrated and he often shut down, believing he was an academic failure. Junior high was an academic nightmare! The incidents are a blur. He has the impression now that he was in the principal's office almost every day. He had problems in reading and writing, and was especially embarrassed when teachers made him read in front of the class. He often coped by being a behavior problem; then he didn't have to read, but it led to the daily encounters with the principal.

High school was much better. His dad was the principal which may have helped his relationships with teachers. He wasn't sure about this since his Dad did not try to give him favors. In fact his father suspended him for chewing tobacco on school property. The suspension was in-house and Jim had to report to school and be confined to a study room. Jim felt he was motivated to succeed academically because of his extracurricular activities. He was on the cross country and track teams so he had to keep his grades up to stay eligible. He loved music and played the trumpet in the symphonic band and orchestra, participating in a musical. He worked hard and felt he was an all-around successful student.

The next educational step was college. West Virginia Wesleyan was a good choice for him. He received support from a caring staff at the Learning Center. He said that he was given a realistic schedule the first semester. It was one in which he could be successful and improve his self-esteem. He particularly appreciated his Western Civilization course as Dr Herbert Coston allowed any student to choose to take oral tests. This was ideal for a dyslexic who could share answers orally much better than writing them. A study skills class, a counselor, and other services of the Learning Center, not only helped him his first semester but also laid the foundation for other successful semesters.

During Jim's senior year, he did his student teaching. His first placement was great, but he had problems with the second placement and his grade was not good. This led to problems with an education professor who was supervising him. She wouldn't change his bad grade and insisted he face the problems he had with this class. He wasn't ready to face those. The situation made him very angry, and he worried that the grade would affect his job opportunities. In retrospect, he looks back at this conflict and appreciates the professor because he knows she helped him to become more realistic about himself.

Upon graduation Jim returned to Florida and accepted a position teaching in Osceola High School, Osceola County, Florida. He taught Learning Strategies, grades 9-12, and was a co-teacher for English, math, and history. He taught there one year, then transferred to Thacker Elementary School, also in Osceola County, where he taught the trainable mentally handicapped and the emotionally handicapped in grades k-5. This was more directly what his major in college had prepared him to do.

Jim gave his all to the students. As a result, after four years he felt burned out. He decided to take a break from teaching and began driving a truck. However, teaching was in his blood. He felt he had to return to the classroom. In 2003 after three years of truck driving, he returned to teaching. He taught Language Arts as the Specific Learning Disabilities teacher in a middle school in Orange County, Florida.

After two years, he transferred to Oak Ridge High School, also in Orange County, where he was the Staffing Specialist for grades 9-12 for 4 years. In this position he was responsible for keeping the school in compliance with the regulations related to teaching learning disabled students. He also had opportunities to counsel students and to do individual work with them, which he thoroughly enjoyed.

Jim always has wanted to keep up with the latest trends and to discover the best methods to teach young people who have different abilities and styles of learning. While at Oak Ridge High School, he finished his Master's Degree in Educational Leadership from Nova Southeastern University in Orlando, Florida. Over the last 15 years he has received certification in Specific Learning Disabilities grades k-12, Varying Exceptionalities grades k-12, Educational Leadership all grades, Multi-subjects grades 1 to 6, and CPR and First Aid. He has continued taking graduate courses at Nova Southeastern University.

ALICE BABSON

Alice's story is both inspirational and challenging. Although she has attention deficit disorder, her major problem is with her eye sight. She only has peripheral vision. This has not stopped her from serving others and pursuing interesting and unusual activities. She could have a "poor me" attitude, but she does not. She meets challenges and seeks interesting activities and ways to serve others. Her loving spirit and concern for others is expressed in all that she does.

Alice Babson's Story

Alice remembers she had teachers she liked in school, but many unhappy experiences as well. She will never forget kindergarten. She had such trouble writing her letters. She wanted to write with her left hand which seemed natural to her, but the teacher insisted she use her right hand. This was a disaster! She'd practice and practice writing her letters, but was seldom successful. As a result the biggest blow came when she was held back in kindergarten and not able to go with her class to first grade. She still remembers with tears in her eyes one of the last days of kindergarten when the class went to visit the first grade room, and she was told to remain in the kindergarten room and practice her letters. What a blow!

In kindergarten and elementary school Alice was a daydreamer. Sometimes she was in her own little world, possibly because she had unhappy experiences in the real world. She liked sports, but wasn't good at them; she often was the last person picked on a team. Her self-esteem was low. She thought the girls in class didn't like her. She remembers kids laughing at her and bouncing a ball off her head. The boys were more friendly and kind.

Alice had physical problems and learning problems. As a result she was placed in the Title One Reading Program (a government program to give individual help in reading.) She doesn't remember being told what her problems were, but remembers stuttering and kids teasing her about this. They also teased her because she had a mole under her nose, and many would laugh and say, "Why don't you get a Kleenex and wipe your nose?" This was painful.

Alice always felt her Dad wanted his first child to be a boy, and she was a disappointment. She wanted to please him so he would be proud of her. She felt she had really found a way to do this when she joined the boy's hockey team in 6th grade and the boy's pre-junior football teams in 7th and 8th grades. She did not play any football in seventh grade, but attended the 7th grade football camp for a month. In eighth grade she was able to play. She had friends among the boys. They respected her as she was the best in calisthenics and a fast runner. The coaches were always kind to her. She is not sure how her dad felt about her playing. He took her to register for the teams, but she remembers other parents who were also registering players acting puzzled or sorry for him that his girl was playing football.

Alice remembers being a lonely child. Since she didn't have many friends, she chose to spend more time with her family. She did not have as much time as she wanted with her dad. He was a well-liked doctor whose work required many hours with his patients. This deprived him of some opportunities to be with Alice and her younger brother. She did enjoy happy times with her mother and particularly remembers the fun they had together making cookies. Another family activity was attending the Episcopal Church together. As a teenager she began making some close friends in her youth group at church. This helped to alleviate her loneliness.

She attended Derby Academy in junior high. It was a very tough school, and Alice worked hard but was greatly stressed. She began to have insomnia which continued through high school. She attended high school at Tabor Academy, a college preparatory school where she continued to struggle and feel stressed as her bouts with insomnia increased.

During her sophomore year she suffered from a virus which lasted about five months. During this time she continued to sleep very little. This lack of sleep may have hindered her body in fighting the virus. As a result the virus caused scar tissue in her central vision. Although her central vision is very poor, she has good peripheral vision. She struggles with vision problems today.

Between high school and college Alice took a year off and lived in Wooster, Massachusetts. During this time she did 5 ten-week internships. The first was at a horseback riding stable where there were 21 horses. She was an assistant teacher helping children learn to ride. In addition she cleaned the horse stalls, which was a hard job. Nevertheless, she enjoyed being near the horses as well as grooming and caring for them.

Her next position was with North East Assistant Dog Service, working with people who were in wheel chairs and those who were deaf. She found it a rather thankless and challenging job as she had to give the dogs commands over and over again. As an intern here, she felt like the lowest person on the totem pole.

Her third position was with The Wooster County Ecumenical Service. This was a clerical position where she interacted with nice people and found it an enjoyable experience. Her fourth position was with an apartment complex for the elderly. Her responsibility was to interview one hundred seventy-five people to gather necessary information for emergencies. She enjoyed talking to the people as she recorded their information. The elderly people liked her and appreciated her willingness to talk with them in a caring manner.

Her fifth position was with a head start organization in an after school family community center. They had programs for day students and after school programs. She worked with children ages 8 to 13, helping to pick them up after school and providing crafts and other activities before assisting in taking them home.

The total year's work was a good learning experience for Alice which she felt prepared her for college. After her acceptance at Wesleyan she was pleased when she received twelve continuing education credit hours for these internships.

She chose West Virginia Wesleyan because she could receive help not only with her attention deficit problem but also with her visual problem. Because of only having peripheral vision, she was classified as legally blind. The learning center provided books from Recordings for the Blind and also had a special reader for her to use.

Wesleyan was the right choice for her. She remembers Dr. Rossbach, a biology professor who taught her so much about plants while making her feel she was an intelligent person. This boosted her self-esteem and self-confidence.

A highlight for Alice was a January trip to Israel which my husband and I led. We were amazed when Alice arrived at the airport with two extra suitcases filled with 30 or 40 pairs of underwear and 60 pairs of jeans! Her minister had shared with the congregation the problems the Palestinians were having. When Alice learned they had a curfew, could not shop, had very low wages, and many restrictions imposed on them, Alice wanted to help. Her church family assisted her with $300.00 to purchase these items. Her minister arranged for a Palestinian to receive the clothes from her. It was a great service project! The airline did not charge her for the extra bags when she explained her purpose.

A highlight of the trip for Alice was her experience in Jerusalem standing on a hill, reciting a poem for us, as we looked over the Kidron Valley. This was an inspirational experience for all of us. Later we stopped in Bethany to see the home of Mary, Martha and Lazarus. The biblical story took on a special meaning for everyone. Alice liked walking with Dr. Thayer White, a retired member of the state department and a retired Wesleyan political science professor. Thayer was not well and had recently lost his wife, Alice. He told many of us that this young Alice with her sensitivity and caring manner was extremely helpful to him during a very difficult time in his life. Alice in turn appreciated that he was a very intelligent man who was able to teach her a great deal. She was glad her name Alice connected them and that she was helpful to him. I was impressed that although Alice was having problems seeing, she covered it up so well that others weren't aware of it.

Alice was always interested in unusual opportunities. In the Spring Semester of 1994, she took a scuba diving class, an unusual opportunity offered at a West Virginia college. There were only eight in the class, two of whom were international students. During the Spring break they went to Key Largo in Florida accompanied by their instructor. The water was warm and Alice enjoyed being there except for a bout of seasickness. After they returned to the college, Alice found the final exam challenging. They swam and had to dive into 38 degree water at Mt. Storm, West Virginia, which was quite a difference from their warm Florida experience.

Alice said one of the best experiences in college was having close friendships for the first time in her life. She was a member of Kappa Phi, a Christian Sorority. This was a group that cared for each other and did service projects for others. She developed friendships which have lasted through the years.

At Wesleyan Alice had double majors: psychology and rehabilitation. She appreciated these majors as she was always a service oriented person. Summer work and a January term experience working at Massachusetts General Hospital gave her opportunities to put her studies into practical experience helping others.

After graduation Alice added to her skills in the summer by taking a nurse's aide course and getting certified as a Nurse's Aide. She also took a three week course at High Point Hospital in High Point, Massachusetts to see if she wanted to enter a program to become a drug counselor. This was an interesting experience and helped her realize that she did not want to become a drug counselor. While studying during the summer, she continued to work as a nurse's aide at the Mayflower Nursing Home.

At the end of the summer, Alice took a leave of absence from the nursing home while she and a college friend camped across the United States from Massachusetts to California. At the end of the journey, her friend flew back and Alice appreciated having an opportunity to stay in California with her grandmother. While there, she took a position as a personal care giver.

Alice knows how to have fun as well as how to work. While she was a care giver for six months, she spent five nights a week doing ball room dancing. She took a dancing class with the Pasadena Ballroom and Dance Association. She then entered the Brown Derby. It was a fun time.

After six months in California, Alice returned to her job as a nurse's aide in Massachusetts. She continued to work for two years, but in 1998 went back to college to study for an associate's degree in science to become an occupational therapist's assistant. On week-ends she worked as a health aide in a Hospice Care Center. In 2000 she received her certification and now works as a certified occupational therapist assistant at May Flower Nursing Home, now known as the Radius Pediatric Health Care Center. She feels her job is all about showing love as well as being kind and caring to her patients.

The Health Care Center serves the behaviorally and mentally disabled. Alice works in their school system with persons age 4 through 22 and with an adult program with adults ranging in age from 22 to 60. This is a challenging career. In addition to her work at the center, she worked for three months in a public school system and then at Lapham Center, a non-profit therapy center working with young people ages 11-22. Alice tries to show love and kindness to all with whom she works.

Because her work is intense, she needs outlets. Since she liked ballroom dancing while in California, she took classes at North Eastern University for a year and a half. She and her boyfriend entered a contest where they competed with others at the bronze level. Although this was fun, she prefers social dancing to competitions.

Another outlet for Alice is traveling. In 2012 she went scuba diving with her boyfriend in Honduras. Her boyfriend, who is also service-oriented, teaches scuba diving. She has taken additional scuba diving lessons since her course at Wesleyan over 18 years ago. It is a sport she enjoys and finds relaxing. It is also an activity she and her boyfriend enjoy together.

I asked Alice for tips that she would give to young people who are physically challenged. She gave the following:

1. Take care of yourself.
2. Keep trying.

3. Follow a path that nurtures your sense of love for yourself, others, and the environment.
4. Remember nothing is ever perfect, just shades of good and bad.
5. Try to accept what you cannot change.
6. Follow your heart.
7. It really helps to believe in God.

Alice Babson, Palestinian bus driver, and Dr. Thayer White

AMY

Amy graduated from West Virginia Wesleyan College in the 1990's as a speech and communications major. She especially enjoyed running, and was a member of the winning Wesleyan Conference Championship Cross Country Team in 1990-1992. She won the conference title in 1992 and went to national three years in a row. She works for the United States Government today.

Amy's Story

Amy struggled with math all her life. She still remembers second grade as a painful time. She couldn't understand subtraction. Amy felt everyone understood the teacher but her. She just couldn't "get it." Finally she was sent to the resource room for additional help, but that was embarrassing for her. She felt "different." She doesn't remember if others teased her, but she inflicted pain on herself. Her parents realized her unhappiness and hired a tutor in the summer to help her. She still appreciates that tutor who helped her understand the basics of math.

Even after tutoring she still found math difficult, but received help. She continued all through elementary school to go to the resource room. In junior high she was in a special learning disabilities class, but in eighth grade she was tested and told that she no longer needed special resources. She qualified to take algebra and geometry in high school in regular classes. However, she remembers struggling. She appreciates her dad who always helped her with algebra homework and organization skills. Algebra II was especially hard for her. She had two teachers during the year. Their different teaching styles made algebra even more confusing. Amy had to attend a special evening class in order to pass. Going to school at night made high school difficult, but she was an avid reader and able to forge ahead in her other subjects.

Because of Amy's struggle with math in high school, her parents felt that she needed to be tested again for a learning disability before she attended college. They were right; she did have a disability. Amy's parents were eager to help her find the right college, one with a special program to meet her needs and especially to receive untimed testing.

Amy was accepted at several colleges, but only West Virginia Wesleyan had the special program she needed. She said, "I knew Wesleyan was right for me." An added attraction was that Wesleyan had a good Cross Country team. Amy loved running. It was her sport in high school. She tried out and was accepted on Wesleyan's track and cross country teams, even gaining a scholarship.

Amy's love for running began in elementary school. Her talent was affirmed in 6th grade when she broke the Presidential Fitness Test Record for running. From then on it was her sport. An added bonus of Wesleyan's cross country team was meeting a fellow runner, Amy Shearman, who was an outstanding runner on the team and also a student in the learning center program. Amy Shearman had worked in a special Learning Center Summer Program for high school juniors, and knew just how to help her new friend Amy. They developed a lasting friendship. Amy enjoyed the cross country team for four years and was thrilled when they won the state conference championship in 1994 and 1995, and then went on to Nationals.

Students who participate in sports have to develop time management skills if they are going to succeed in college. This is especially true with anyone who has any type of learning problem. Amy realized this. In the summer between high school and college, she bought and listened to the tape, *"Where There's a Will There's an A"*, which helped prepare her for college. She was a pleasure to have in my study skills class because she was eager to learn all the tips that would help her become the best student she could be.

Graduating from Wesleyan with a major in speech communication and dramatic arts plus a minor in music, opened several doors for jobs. She began by working as an intern on WUSA Channel 9 TV station in Washington, DC. She enjoyed the work, but realized she needed to move on to a better paying job. She accepted a position as a receptionist/administrative assistant in a law firm where she worked for four years. Amy has always had a passion to help with the environment, and was thrilled when the opportunity came for her to work for a government environmental/energy contractor, supporting The Assistant Deputy for the Under Secretary of Defense for Installations and Environment. In this position she had opportunities to attend conferences all over the United States in order to give the under secretary ideas for saving energy. Her work was very fulfilling as she knew she was helping her country and the world. Five years later another opportunity came and she accepted a position with a government contractor supporting Department of Defense (DOD.)

While in college, Amy not only enjoyed running, but also singing in the Chapel Choir. Today she is a singer in her church choir. She also continues running. She found it awesome to participate in the Marine Corp Marathon. She ran for a charity to help raise funds for AIDS and through this group received free training for her financial support. They were sponsored by the Whitman-Walker Clinic. Her future plans are to participate in the Dewey Beach Sprint Triathlon and to continue to excel at work and accept new challenges to grow.

Amy has a good philosophy of life: "Balance your work life with personal life and don't live to work but work to live and focus on others."

Amy shared the following tips for others:

1. Don't freak out about your difficulties, but figure out how to compensate.
2. Remember we all learn differently.
3. Pursue your dreams.

4. Be positive.
5. Don't let others stop you. They may have their own issues.
6. Don't let a disability prevent you from reaching your goal.
7. Keep plugging along.
8. Reach for the stars and you'll just fall short of the moon.
9. Make sure you define God's purpose for your life. Faith can produce miracles.

MATTHEW WALLACE

Matthew Wallace is a gifted artist, blacksmith, founder and co-owner of Wallace Metal Works in Charleston, West Virginia. His parents have always been very supportive of him, and his whole family is very caring. Like many dyslexics his story is one of pain, challenges, and perseverance leading to success.

Matthew "Matt" Wallace's Story

Matt's problem began in first grade when he had difficulty reading. This was hard for Matt to understand, and it surprised his teacher since his kindergarten records were good. Both his teacher and parents realized he was not able to read material he had read in kindergarten. His parents were concerned and had him tested which proved he was above average in intelligence but had a learning disability, dyslexia.

As a result of the first grade experience and the testing, Matt's parents and teacher knew he needed to have summer learning experiences to reinforce his learning. Realizing he had a reading problem was a painful experience for him, especially since his problem meant that summers would never be the same. Every summer while he was in elementary school, he had to attend the Swain Learning Center in St Albans, a nearby town. He remembers that it was bad enough having to go to school, but driving there was not pleasant as they had to drive past a smelly chemical center which Matt called "PU City." Despite his negative feelings, he realizes that his mother tried to make it enjoyable by stopping for fast food, buying match box cars, or providing other treats and surprises.

This was the period in our history when many people did not understand learning disabilities and even questioned their existence. His mother was a "cooperative advocate" and worked with the teachers helping them understand Matt and his problem. Matt attended The River School, which was an ideal place for him because it had an open curriculum, small classes (8-15 children), and no letter grades.

Junior High at a Catholic School was more regimented and harder for Matt to be accepted and achieve. He had a teacher who didn't believe in learning disabilities and would give no accommodations. His mother had to change from the "cooperative advocate" to become an "aggressive advocate" telling the teacher that giving accommodations was the law. Her words fell on deaf ears. His mother became more determined to do something when the private counselor who was working with Matt told her to get him out of that school before Matt wants to kill you for putting him there. His parents took the counselor's advice and began looking for a private school. They chose Forman School in Litchfield, Connecticut, a school for dyslexics.

Forman was the right choice for Matt. Teachers appreciated him and his ability. When he wanted to read *War and Peace* in ninth grade, his teacher in his one-on-one language arts class changed her teaching plans and they read it together. The next year she followed with his choice of *Gone with the Wind*. These were challenging books but he was able to earn a B in the class. Although he excelled at the school and appreciated the caring teachers, he had periods of homesickness. He really wanted to be closer to home. Since he had enough hours for graduation, but lacked only an English and history requirement, the parents pursued the idea of entering West Virginia Wesleyan and taking the two requirements his freshman year.

This was an unusual request especially from a dyslexic student. The director of admissions talked with me and we decided to consider their request depending on Matt's progress in our LD summer program requiring a college level class. Matt made an A in Introduction to

Psychology and was admitted to Wesleyan as a freshman and part of Wesleyan's Special Support Program. His freshman English course and first history class met Foreman's requirements for graduation.

Matt loved art and majored in it; but his father wanted him to have another major so that he could get a "real job." Since his other love was history, he had a double major: history and art. He enjoyed college, but remembers one painful experience. An art professor, who did not agree with the college's policy of allowing LD students to take their exams untimed, would not allow Matt to do this. However, Matt stood up to her telling her that under the Americans With Disabilities Act he could do this. At the end of the period he walked out taking his exam to the Learning Center where he finished it and made a B+ or A- on the exam.

Following graduation from college, Matt's dad encouraged him to become certified as an insurance agent and use his art major as an avocation. After a year working in insurance he knew he did not want to have an insurance career. Art was his love, especially blacksmithing. After taking a year's apprenticeship in Goshen, Connecticut, he knew this was his passion, but still worried about it becoming his profession.

Matt's interest in blacksmithing began when he was 11 or 12. His parents had hired a blacksmith, Jeff Fetty, to do some work for them. Matt became fascinated by what Jeff was doing and followed him around. Jeff, seeing his interest, invited Matt to his shop where he had an incredible time. This was the beginning of his dream. While in college Matt did an internship with Jeff, further pursuing this dream.

Today, Matt's partner in his business is his wife, Tessie. They are a wonderful couple complimenting each other with their skills. Tessie was a trained bench jeweler and this talent enabled her to weld iron. She has business and computer experience which has allowed them to use technology to expand their business. Both Matt and Tessie are juried artists with Tamarack, an art and craft center featuring "The Best of West Virginia."

Matt has not limited his study of blacksmithing to the United States. He went with a group of blacksmiths led by Leonard Masters to

Germany, France, and Spain to study work there. His mentor, Jeff Fetty, was also part of the trip. He and Tessie have also gone to Bologna, Italy, where Tessie had studied previously. As a result of Tessie's searching on line, they have visited and spent time with a well-known Blacksmith, Pierluigi Prata, a third generation blacksmith who was given the award of Maestro d'Arte by the city of Bologna. Matt accepted his invitation to apprentice with him at his shop, Bottega Prata, for seventeen days in September, 2011.

Throughout all his experiences Matt is grateful for his happy, loving home and the support of his parents. He appreciates the opportunity they gave him to go to Forman School. As a child his dad taught him to work with boats and he and his siblings had fun with him on Saturdays. His mother is a caring, loving person who was always there to support him. She was a task master. When he didn't want to go to college and at those times when he wanted to quit, she helped him persevere. She told him, "Someday before you are thirty, Matthew, you will thank me for this." When he was 22 or 23 he said, "Thank you, Mom."

Matt and Tessie have found careers that they both love. They design and forge one of a kind custom iron works, making creations such as handrails, lanterns, gates, terrace railings, balconies, headboards, and small items like birds, fish, leaves and flowers. They can make almost anything a customer desires. Matt has succeeded in what seemed like "the impossible dream."

Matt's Tips for Young People

1. Dyslexia can be a gift.
2. If you don't go through something, you can't identify with problems brought out by adversity.
3. Appreciate the educational world. Take time to read and study.
4. Choose a career in which you have a passion and enjoy it.

Celebration of Success | 141

Tess and Matt

ROBERT HOGAN

The life of Robert Hogan is a good example of overcoming difficulties through study and hard work. Currently, he is a Commissioner in the Maryland judicial system. His story is an inspiration to others.

Robert "Rob" Hogan's Story

Rob's home was near Mt. Dora, Florida, a little town north of Orlando. He lived with his mother and grandparents and considers himself a country boy who loved to fish, hunt, and enjoy the out-of-doors. From his grandfather he learned to work hard—farming, working in the orange groves, and even learning about the plumbing business. It was not only important to work hard at home, but also to work hard at school. His family was supportive, always trying to help him with his school work. He remembers the painful experience of being "held back" to repeat third grade. He always wanted to be the same or better than others, but this experience made him feel he was not. He had failed to meet his and his family's expectation and he didn't understand why.

Sixth grade was also a painful time as the teacher reported to his family that he was reading on the third grade level. He feels this was a curve ball thrown at him. He felt he wasn't as good as his classmates, and began asking himself, "What is the matter with me?" His teachers and his family also had trouble understanding why he couldn't achieve. They knew he was motivated and hard working. Learning disabilities often were not understood in the early 1980's. Wanting to help, his family took action and enrolled him in a private school that had a home based curriculum. Although his classes were small and his teachers provided more individual attention, he still found school difficult. His family tried hard to help him, but all of them continued to be frustrated.

When Rob was ready for high school, his family wanted him to have a good experience and a top notch education. His aunt and uncle in Miami, Florida, suggested he live with them and attend an all-male Marist Brothers Catholic School. It was a wonderful school and he achieved academically. He felt he grew in spirit, mind, and body. He worked hard and had caring teachers who helped him realize he could achieve. His teachers recognized that he wanted to learn and was motivated to work hard. He played football which taught him lessons about working with others and the importance of being a team player. He was very good and he dreamed of attending a Division I university and eventually being part of the NFL.

During his junior year, he was tested and it was discovered that he had a learning disability, dyslexia, which affected his reading, writing, and memory. It was helpful for him to finally understand why he had been having problems. As a result of the diagnosis, he then received private support including counseling and tutoring. This helped prepare him for college.

Counselors in the private agency and teachers in his high school helped him as he looked ahead to college. He applied and was accepted at The Universities of Louisiana, Alabama, Minnesota, and West Virginia, all good Division I schools. However, his coach and teachers encouraged him to attend West Virginia Wesleyan for two reasons: In football at a smaller school he would probably play as a starter his freshman year. He was encouraged "to be a big fish in a little pond rather than a little fish in a big pond." The clincher was that the Wesleyan Learning Center's support program was ranked number one in the nation for students with learning disabilities. Rob knew he could receive the help he needed there. He wanted to be a good student and succeed academically, as well as become an outstanding football player.

He attended Wesleyan and just as Miami had been a culture shock from Mt Dora, Buckhannon was a culture shock from Miami. However, he liked the small town where everyone said hello, and the friendly college atmosphere where professors cared about him. Brian Jozwiak, an assistant coach, was always positive and accepting. He is a person whom Rob will never forget. Rob appreciated the services of the Learning Center. The recorded text books, tutors, note takers, and a caring staff were just what he needed. He appreciated the Lindamood-Bell ® Program, especially the Visualizing Verbalizing, a method developed by Nanci Bell of California. This method allowed him to visualize the material and use his great gift of memory to verbalize it in his writing and reading. Rob finally became a good reader. He still uses this method today. Rob was a good student and an outstanding football player. He developed an interesting study method which he still uses today.

Rob says his greatest experience at Wesleyan was meeting his wife, Emily. They studied together in the Learning Center and dated all through college. Emily became an outstanding teacher, whose story is also included in this book.

In addition to studying and playing football, Rob was willing to help others. He was a student leader in Wesleyan's summer program for high school juniors with learning disabilities. He helped the students develop methods of learning and to believe in themselves.

After graduation in 1997, it was time to pursue his dream of becoming an NFL football player. Although he participated in professional combines including the NFL combine, and practiced with two teams, the big opportunity did not come. It was a major disappointment. As a result, he knew it was time to decide about his future.

He pursued graduate work and completed 26 hours toward a Master of Science degree from Lynn University, specializing in Health Care Administration. During his internship he worked in a nursing home, which was both a good and bad experience. He became upset when he realized that administrators were more concerned about making money than the care and welfare of the patients. He knew he had to look elsewhere for his life long career.

Emily, his college girlfriend and future wife, was with him in Florida. When she accepted a teaching job in Maryland, he followed her there.

After working several years for the state port authority, Rob enrolled in the Commissioners Academy. There he found his calling to become part of the judicial system where he has had a very successful career for more than ten years.

Rob's Tips for Others with LD:

1. Explore your interests and dreams.
2. See what works for you.

EMILY PATTON HOGAN

Emily Hogan is a first grade teacher who knows the importance of helping children believe they can succeed. She strives to meet her students' needs by individualizing her work with them and showing them she cares. She is married to Robert Hogan, whose story also appears in this book.

Emily Patton Hogan's Story

Emily's learning disabilities, visual special processing and attention deficit disorder (ADD), were not diagnosed until her sophomore or junior year in high school. She has unpleasant memories of elementary and middle school, before she knew what was wrong. Although she tried and worked hard, she only made C's or D's, but her sister who didn't study made A's. This was painful and frustrating, especially when she couldn't understand why. Her teachers often thought she was lazy or didn't care due to her lack of concentration and day dreaming. The teacher would be talking and Emily was looking at the teacher's pretty red fingernails or was distracted by the movie next door which could be heard in an open class room. This is behavior which is typical of an ADD child, but many teachers didn't know about ADD in the early 1980's.

Her behavior in class did not prepare her for homework. She remembers her parents thinking she was rebellious, and she now believes they were right. Her mother would send her to the home office to study. Since she was rebelling, she didn't want to study and really didn't know how to study effectively. She spent most of her time just looking at the pages. She did poorly on tests, and remembers often being "grounded" because her parents were upset with her grades. She hated school.

In eighth grade her parents enrolled her in a private school where there were smaller classes and opportunities for extra help. She attended this school through 12th grade. However, she still had problems especially with reading and taking tests. Her parents hired tutors, but they really didn't understand she needed to learn differently. Telling her, "Read the page," wasn't the answer to her problems.

Emily applied to West Virginia Wesleyan where she and her parents interviewed with me. Her parents appreciated the interview because I told them we would help Emily understand how her brain works and teach the best ways for her to learn.

Although Emily wanted to attend a large university, Wesleyan was the right school for her. During her freshman year she learned ways to study effectively, and began to understand her learning style. The Lindamood-Bell ® reading program where she learned to visualize as she read helped her finally improve her reading comprehension. Also, she could choose the particular services of the Learning Center which met her needs.

Emily entered college planning to major in psychology, preparing for a career in child psychology using her skills to work with children and young people. After one semester she realized psychology wasn't her field. She decided to take classes in education. She enjoyed these classes and knew this was the right field for her.

After graduation, she moved to Florida to be with Robert Hogan, her boyfriend from college. She began working in a private preschool and kindergarten. Although she enjoyed her teaching, when an opportunity came for her to teach in Bowie, Maryland, her home state, she took a kindergarten position there. After teaching two years, her parents encouraged her to go on to graduate school. She could take one course at a time and still teach. Emily enjoyed her classes and the opportunity to do projects and relate them to her teaching. She appreciated her professors who understood the importance of flexibility in assessment and teaching. She received her Master of Arts in Reading Education from Bowie State University.

While teaching and doing graduate work, she married her college sweetheart, Rob Hogan. He had followed her to Maryland and began working there.

Many young adults with learning disabilities fear educational challenges. Emily had lived through many bad experiences before becoming a teacher. However, the challenges of teaching and learning motivated her to tackle another opportunity: the challenge to receive a National Teacher's Certificate. Her school district offered scholarships and salary incentives to teachers who would apply. She and three of her colleagues decided to try.

The National Teacher's Certification program was difficult. She received a portfolio in October and had to finish it by March with very little direction. She and her friends called it the "national puzzle with no answer key." It required a lot of self-reflection; it focused on how you are teaching, working with parents, workshops, and everything you do that affects your students. After completing her portfolio in March, it was sent to readers around the country, and she did not hear anything until November. She needed a score of 141. When she checked on line to find her score, she was devastated. Her score was 140, only one point away! She had been an A student on her Master's degree courses, but now another failure. Memories of the past came flooding through her mind. Two of her other friends also failed. Only one of her colleagues passed.

At first Emily was ready to throw in the towel. She had tried, worked hard, but failed. She was LD; what could she expect? However, with encouragement from others, she did not give up. Since there was a three year period to work toward passing the test, the school district was supportive of the teachers who were willing to try again. They received scholarships and "went for it." Since there was no feedback, it was difficult to know how to improve. Scores on each area were given as a way for her to assess her work. Her approach was to study the scores and decide how to undertake each task. She tackled the science area which was the lowest and *passed*! She became only the 35th teacher in her county to achieve this goal. The National Teacher's certification allows her to teach anywhere in the United States.

Another success story is her teaching. Emily remembers painful experiences she had in school because she needed to have teachers who individualized class lessons and gave different types of assessment. She doesn't want "her children" to have the same experience. She knows it is difficult to individualize when you have 23 in a class room, but she tries. She also knows one test doesn't fit all, and works with different modes of assessment. She wants "her children" to feel success and to believe in themselves. She loves her students and they know she cares about them. Emily told me, "I can't imagine doing anything else but teaching."

Emily's Tips

1. Don't be discouraged.
2. Learn what works for you.
3. Don't be afraid to say "I'm not getting it." Ask for help.
4. Find your nitch. "What are you strong in?"
5. Don't let anything stop you.
6. Find a person you can trust.
7. Don't give up.

CHRISTOPHER KELLOGG

"Chris Kellogg is one of the most caring persons I know. You need to write about him." This was shared with me by a Wesleyan Alum. After interviewing Chris, I knew this was true. Chris is a social worker whose specialty is geriatrics. He comes from a very supportive family. He graduated from West Virginia Wesleyan in 1998.

Christopher "Chris" Kellogg's Story

Chris works at Raritan Health Clinic in New Jersey. This health facility is known not only for its good health care but also for its caring and concern for patients. Some elderly persons when needing services tell their care givers, "Take me to Chris's place." Chris provides both physical and social services including counseling and general information to help persons recover. If they need long term care, he recommends places where they can receive services. He advises and challenges them to go forward with a positive attitude.

Possibly one of the reasons that Chris has the reputation for being caring is his appreciation for people who supported, cared, and were concerned about him. He had an automobile accident while in junior high school. This was a terrible time for him. He said when he thinks about Kim Baker, a social worker who helped him after the accident, he gets "goose bumps." As a result of the accident, he knew he could no longer be the "big jock", but would walk with a limp the rest of his life. Kim Baker tutored him all summer, making him realize he could go forward and do well.

Chris is dyslexic and reading was always a big challenge for him before and after the accident. Math and writing were also problems that he had to face. His mother is his hero. She was always there to support him. This meant extra help, tutoring, and even suing the school system.

Chris's parents felt that he would have better experiences in high school if he attended Forman, a private school in Litchfield, Connecticut, specializing in teaching dyslexic young people. Chris was able to start as a day student but later felt he would gain more by living on campus. The atmosphere at Forman included quality teaching and small classes which were ideal for him. He particularly profited by the reading support. He was prepared for college, and West Virginia Wesleyan was the right school for him. Here he not only received good teaching but also he continued to receive the reading support needed for success in school. He was a good all-around student and became president of his junior class.

Chris remembers caring teachers at Wesleyan. He entered college knowing he needed to continue his reading development and was very anxious about his math skills. He realized he had obstacles to overcome but he had the Kellogg "I can do it" attitude. He found teachers who recognized his determination and went the extra mile to help. Chris says professors Howard Bright, Ruth Calef, Becky Gurdak, Phyllis Coston, and other Learning Center staff members not only taught him, but also were patient and challenged him to excel. They helped him adjust his schedule to be able to meet college requirements and build on his strengths not his weaknesses. In graduate school, Dr. Botnick also stands out as helpful and caring. We sometimes forget how important teachers are in the lives of students. Chris remembers the positive teachers; but he also remembers those teachers who were negative. There was a teacher in junior high that made fun of him when he pushed the wrong button three times in a computer science class. To this day he recalls the teacher asking him, "Are you stupid?" Negative remarks by teachers are usually not forgotten.

After graduation, Chris took a year off school to earn money before attending Boston University where he received a Master's degree in Social Work with a concentration in gerontology. He was an outstanding student and received the Award for Excellence in gerontology, given by the gerontology department to a student who shows current and future dedication to the elderly. His gerontology department was right; he is dedicated to the elderly. In his current position he helps the elderly in many ways.

In 2004 Chris married DeeDee, a hydro geologist. They have two children who enrich their lives and whom they thoroughly enjoy.

Chris's Tips

1. Don't run from challenges you face. Acknowledge them and do something.
2. Maximize your strengths and minimize your weaknesses.
3. Be your own self advocate.
4. Talk to your teachers.
5. Get the type of support you need, such as tutors, etc.
6. Be proud you are dyslexic!

CATHERINE ELDRIDGE

Catherine Eldridge believes in living life to its fullest! She is a graphic designer who enjoys her work for a government agency, but takes advantages of life's opportunities which include traveling, mountain climbing, and running.

Catherine "Katie" Eldridge's Story

Katie remembers elementary school as a frustrating time. She wasn't a trouble maker and she tried hard to achieve, but her grades were poor. Finally in fourth grade her teacher recommended to her parents that she be tested. Her parents wanted to know what the problem was. The results indicated she had an auditory memory problem and a mild case of dyslexia. It really was a relief to discover this and learn how she could receive help. She was able to remain in her classes, but go to the resource room for extra help one period each day.

Teachers play a key role in a student's achieving and feeling successful. After Katie was tested, she remembers a teacher who was particularly helpful. When the class had to rewrite ten sentences, the teacher put a magnet beside the number of the one sentence that was her goal to achieve. It was realistic and she could do it. This is a good strategy and highly recommended to teachers today. Katie's parents not only were aware of her learning needs, but also her learning style. Knowing she was both a visual and a tactile learner, they realized experiential learning would be the best for her. They traveled to many historical places and visited numerous museums. Katie feels these were great learning experiences and helped her in classes as well as preparing her for the future.

In addition to enrichment experiences, her parents provided other opportunities for support. These included tutors, SAT preparation, and attendance at the Britannica Learning Center where she received help in learning her basic fundamentals. Her dad was particularly understanding of her problems and needs because he had similar problems in a time when help was not given or available to students who learned differently. Another helpful opportunity came when a high school teacher offered extra credit for someone to work once a week at an art gallery. Katie was always eager to improve her grades and volunteered. It was a wonderful experience and she continued volunteering all through high school. It probably influenced her later career choice.

Despite the fact that the Fairfax School System was very good and she is appreciative of all the support she received, like most LD students she had some problems. She will never forget some students in the gifted program asking her if her parents got her brains at K Mart, and a teacher in 7th or 8th grade telling her that she would never amount to anything. These unkind remarks which last a lifetime were very painful to her. She was very sensitive and wanted to learn. She wanted her brain to be like others.

Although tests and academic work were difficult, she found an outlet where she could succeed—The Cross Country Team. She could run and not worry about spelling, etc.; she could participate with her fellow team members and win. It helped her accept herself and realize she could succeed.

Katie continued with cross country when she came to Wesleyan. She made many friends on the team and had successful seasons. She also joined Zeta Tau Alpha and loved her sorority sisters. She majored in graphic design and minored in anthropology. Katie took courses in anthropology because she enjoyed the professor, Dr. Fred Peterson. She especially liked his stories which helped her remember her early experiences with her parents visiting historical places.

Katie advises other learning disabled youth to use all the resources a college offers. She felt tutors, note takers, and taking tests on the computer were so helpful to her success in college. She was particularly grateful that she had to rework her class notes in the Learning Center because the center believed reworking them was much better for learning than receiving a Xeroxed copy.

Katie graduated from Wesleyan in 1998, and began working for Price Waterhouse Coopers as a production coordinator for their in-house graphic design studio. She transferred to other positions in the company, and when IBM bought out the consulting practice, she worked for them. Later she began working for the government.

Katie has enjoyed her professional career, but she has especially appreciated opportunities to travel and see the world. In 2001 she went trekking in the Khumbu Region of Nepal, climbing Mount Everest and successfully making it to the Everest Base Camp. Nepal was a wonderful learning experience! It was really the first time she was actually out of her comfort zone. She was experiencing a different culture, different language, different religion, and learning in a way that fitted her learning style. She was impressed with the people, especially the "street kids." Since the young people from Nepal wanted to learn English, they met with the young people from the tour group. In the evenings, they practiced their English by asking all kinds of questions. Katie was particularly impressed that they knew so much about President Bush, political events, and various problems.

Preparing for a trip like this does not happen overnight. Katie saved up her vacation time, got an evening job at an equipment store where she could receive a discount on her purchases, and saved her money. She looked for a travel agency with whom she could travel safely as a single woman.

Nepal created an appetite for more international experiences. In 2005 she trekked up Mt. Kilimanjaro in Tanzania. Katie has a spirit for adventure and believes in taking advantage of opportunities. Therefore, before meeting her group in Tanzania she stopped in Amsterdam for two days. She wanted to visit art museums, but finding places when you don't speak the language often becomes an adventure. She took the wrong train going the wrong direction but still had a good time. People are always willing to help a lost American.

Amsterdam was fun, but climbing Mt Kilimanjaro was wonderful! Meeting people in local villages opened her eyes to understanding how other people live. She joined the villagers and learned to rely on drinking water from snow. With the help of the guides and some of the residents, she was able to learn a few words in Swahili and with gestures was able to communicate. A cold prevented her from reaching the summit, but she climbed 18,000 feet and will never forget the experience.

Mountain climbing gets in your blood, and Katie has continued to climb. In 2007 she tackled Mt. Rainer on a charity climb, "Summit for Someone." The goal was to raise money to help inner city children get out of the city for the summer. During the same summer, she climbed above the tree line at Mt. St. Helen. This allowed her to see tremendous growth and other changes which have occurred since the volcano's eruption in May, 1980.

Besides saving and earning money for mountain climbing experiences, keeping in shape is very important. Running was her natural sport. In 2002 she ran her first Marine Corp Marathon and her second in 2005. Since her dad was a marathon runner they ran together. He ceremoniously ran the first mile with her to encourage her, but then he took off. Running with him was a thrill as she had watched him run marathons for years. She knew he would cross the finish line, but they both were ecstatic when she crossed it, too.

Katie enjoys new experiences and thrives on opportunities. She now owns a Siberian husky and belongs to a Siberian Husky Club in Pennsylvania. Despite the fact that she calls her husky a couch potato, she races him all over the East Coast.

Katie's belief about taking advantage of opportunities is not limited to personal experiences. For instance, she entered a program at work to study to be an analytical writer. She loves her profession as a graphic designer and has no desire to change jobs. She just welcomes opportunities to learn. It is with this spirit of adventure and motivation for learning that she shares the following tips for other LD persons.

Katie's Tips

1. Don't miss opportunities given to you in life or work, even when they don't seem relevant to your current work.
2. If there is something you want to do in life, don't hesitate—do it.
3. Don't turn down help.

PATRICIA BOOTHE

Patricia Boothe grew up in Salem, Virginia, with very supportive parents but a school system which was not. She has been a special education teacher for over eleven years in that same school district which is now extremely supportive. She has touched the lives of many children including autistic children. Her story is an inspiration to others.

Patricia "Tricia" Boothe's Story

Patricia started school as a happy bright little girl. Very soon she was having some problems and her parents realized that something was interfering with her learning process. When she was in second grade, her parents discussed her problems with a teacher who was a family friend. She suggested that Tricia be tested. The parents immediately went to the school with this suggestion; but when given the minimal tests, Tricia's parents were told she did not qualify for services. Like many girls who were pleasant and behaved well during the 1980's, teachers did not consider her a child with problems and refused to have her tested further even though her parents kept saying that there was something wrong as she still had reading problems. "Give her time, it will happen," they were told. It did not happen!

Tricia remembers her fourth and fifth grade years as miserable times. She was very frustrated. She knew something was wrong. She worked hard wanting to learn to read well and to understand the material. Her parents believed her, but the teachers did not. "Try harder," the teachers said. But she still could not process information no matter how hard she tried. The more she tried the more frustrated she became.

Middle school was even worse. Every day she heard, "You are not studying enough. You need to try harder." Her mom and dad attended parent teacher conferences and heard the same remarks. They were told, "She is a sweet child, but she needs to study and practice more." Her parents explained that she knew the information when studying at home, and she worked hard every evening. Something was happening between home and school. Tricia thinks today it had something to do with her processing. Finally, in middle school her parents decided to "take a back seat." The nightly battles had made home life miserable. Since Tricia just hated school, her parents knew she needed a happy home environment.

When Tricia was in high school, she had one of the worst experiences of her school years. The guidance counselor told her that she wasn't college material and enrolled her in vocational and general studies classes. She went home and cried, sharing with her parents that she wanted to take pre-college English and other college preparatory classes. Although she explained this to her guidance counselor, the counselor would not put her in those classes. Her parents knew it was time for them to take action again. They told the counselor that if she couldn't enroll her in those classes, they would go to someone who could! "She is going to take those classes, and if she fails them we will deal with that when it happens," they said. When Tricia's parents forced the school to have her enrolled in pre-college courses, Spanish I was a problem for her. Tricia scored a 46% on the written portion of the first exam and a 98% on the oral portion of this same exam. Her parents knew this wasn't right. Her mother went to the school and requested that someone explain how she could make such a discrepancy in her scores. She was told, "Obviously, she knows the material but can't put it in writing." The parents again not only requested that she be retested, but this time they insisted on it. Tricia's father took on the advocacy role which many parents often feel they have to do and said, "I want her given the full battery of tests right away. You should have done this years ago, but you put us off. We are not waiting any longer, as she clearly needs help."

Tricia was in ninth grade when she was tested, and the results indicated that she had processing problems. The school developed strategies for her. Her IEP (Individual Educational Plan) indicated that she needed extended time for tests and needed to be placed under the care of a special education teacher. Hearing her IEP was a relief to her; but she feared being separated from friends and put in special education classes. Instead she was placed in the college preparatory classes. Her mother had a written copy of the IEP so she went to a resource teacher when needed. The school was not equipped to have a student leave the class room for extended time on tests and at first was not going to permit this. Her dad, a lawyer and a determined advocate, went to the school pointing out that the IEP was a legal document and had to be enforced. He suggested she take the exam in another room and return to class afterwards.

After Tricia received the needed accommodations, she liked high school better. For many of her elective classes, she had a background for the information and an interest which made the work easier. She still had trouble with auditory processing and reading. She read slowly and usually had to read material over and over again to comprehend it. This is a common problem among slow readers. Brain research has taught us that the short term memory can hold only seven items. When persons are reading long sentences very slowly, they forget the beginning of the sentence, making comprehension difficult. This was certainly true in Tricia's case.

Between her junior and senior year of high school, Tricia attended Wesleyan's summer program. As a requirement of this program, she took a college class, Introduction to Psychology. When she did well and passed the course, she and her parents were thrilled. They had been right! She could do college work and high school college preparatory classes were right for her.

When Tricia came to Wesleyan she was relieved; she was no longer a guinea pig. Accommodations were in place and her parents did not need to fight for her. She met many students with similar problems and she didn't feel different taking tests and receiving help. The pressures and stress she had in high school were gone. She did, however, begin medication. Her parents had avoided it in high school where they could help her; but as an independent student, she needed it. Her college grade point average went up from 2.5 to 3.0. In reflecting on her educational experiences, Tricia said some of her best experiences were at Wesleyan. The Lindamood-Bell ® Reading Program was particularly beneficial because it helped her with her processing problems. It was so valuable to her that after she began teaching, she persuaded her school to use parts of it. She also encouraged her parents to use part of it for her younger sister who also had processing problems. Tricia's years in college were enjoyable and seemed to go fast; but she was eager to begin teaching.

In May 1999, she graduated from Wesleyan and immediately signed up to be a substitute teacher in her home town of Salem, VA. Three days later, before she was even finished unpacking, she received a call to substitute. It is a day she won't forget! She was on the playground when a fifth grade special education student whom she had been teaching before recess, started a fight. She immediately confronted him and settled the fight. Another teacher watching her said, "O my gosh! I can't believe he is listening to you!" That afternoon the principal asked her to come in the next day to set up an interview for a position. Within a few days she was offered a regular teaching position at the school where she had subbed.

This was the beginning of her career at South Salem Elementary School where she began as a primary special education teacher. South Salem is part of the Salem City School System where she had attended. In 2003, the school system recognized an overwhelming need for teaching children on the autism spectrum. Tricia's classroom was restructured, and she began teaching in the newly refocused developmental delay classroom which was devoted to teaching children with autism, spectrum disorders, and developmental delays.

Tricia taught autistic children for seven years and was very effective. During that time an article appeared in the *Salem Times Register* describing her teaching and the extraordinary program for students with special needs. Parents were thrilled that children who were non-verbal began to communicate with them in sentences. Some of the autistic children were able to move up to regular classrooms for part or all of the day. Several techniques made Tricia successful with the children. These included being flexible and individualizing children's work. Each child knew he or she was special and she met their individual needs in a caring manner, giving children positive reinforcement when they answered questions correctly.

The article in the *Salem Times Register* stated, "Each child carries a picture schedule that breaks up tasks into a series of steps." It went on to say that Patricia prepared children for field trips in a special way, allowing them to see pictures of persons they would see and what they would be expected to do. To reinforce this, Tricia kept a key chain on her ID badge to remind them of whom they were going to see and what they were going to do next.

In the fall of 2010, Tricia moved in to a regular kindergarten classroom. Special education classes come with the same commitment as teaching regular classes, but with a great deal of additional stress. Because of the long hours of required paper work and time consuming hours of meetings after school, she felt it was time for her to make a change. Tricia also felt that the change would enable her to reach all different kinds of learners and share her own experiences and learning strategies with the regular education population. It was, however, bittersweet to her. She will always cherish the time she spent teaching and relating to the children in need of special education. She laughs as she says, "Who knows, maybe one day I'll go back."

Tricia's teaching career has been in the same city where she had so many problems getting her needs met as a student. She is very pleased that attitudes and ways of teaching learning disabled children have changed so dramatically.

Tricia's Tips for LD Students

1. "No" is not acceptable. You have to find ways to make things work.
2. Be an advocate for yourself and do it in a way that shows you have confidence in yourself.

JACK EWING

Phyllis Coston and Jack Ewing

When Jack learned that Albert Einstein was dyslexic, like him, it was the beginning of a new perspective on his problems. Dyslexia has caused Jack many painful experiences which he finds difficult to discuss without tears. However, he now calls his dyslexia "an uncommon gift." Jack is a 1995 graduate of West Virginia Wesleyan College who is a successful chemist with U.S. Steel today.

Jack's Story

Jack has always had unpleasant memories of school. His problems began in first grade when he felt embarrassed because he had trouble reading, writing, and spelling. Fortunately he had an experienced, caring teacher who recognized he was a very intelligent child and should not be struggling. At the end of first grade she recommended Jack be tested.

Jack was tested at the beginning of second grade. The newly appointed assistant superintendent of schools was dyslexic, and was not only willing but eager to help struggling children. The school district hired a psychologist from the University of Pittsburgh to test Jack. The psychologist was impressed with Jack, and said he was the most "cultured second grader" she had seen. The first grade teacher's recognition of a problem was correct. Jack was dyslexic and also gifted. As a result, he was placed in both the special education class and the gifted class.

Jack feels being dyslexic was a disadvantage all through school. He compared it to racial discrimination. He was always in the minority and received comments similar to racial slurs from peers and some adults. He remembers being called dumb or stupid especially when he went to the special education class. I asked him if these remarks were made by members of his gifted class. He said no. Socially the gifted students were his best friends. However, despite the good experiences in the gifted class, he said elementary school was one failure after another.

He had terrible experiences in fourth grade. His teacher did not understand him or dyslexia and did not want to give accommodations. He was humiliated many times. His hatred of his fourth grade teacher is so strong that his family will not speak about it in front of him today because it is too painful.

He was glad to move to junior high and later high school. There he was no longer in a self-contained classroom with one teacher. Moving to different classes meant that students were unaware that he was attending a special education class. However, he had one painful situation in tenth grade. When he asked the teacher to send his test the next day to the special education classroom, she berated him before the whole class saying he was trying to change the curve on the test by getting special privileges. He was very embarrassed especially since up to this time he thought most of his classmates did not know he was dyslexic. He couldn't concentrate the rest of the class period and felt most of the students were staring at him. He cried when he shared the experience with his mother. She was supportive of him and arranged for a special parent-teacher conference.

Although he found this to be an extremely painful experience, he appreciates the good teachers who were supportive and accepted him. His middle school special education teacher was helpful by encouraging him to accept and respect himself. He said this teacher always began class with encouraging words, and he would think to himself, "Wow, she understands us." He will never forget her! In high school he had a wonderful biology teacher whose classes were exciting and challenging. He paid close attention to her and her teaching methods. One day Jack had a slip of the tongue and said to her: "You are dyslexic." She was surprised at his statement but shared that she was dyslexic. He said that he put his head down and said, "I knew it, I knew it, I knew it." It was important for him to know she was dyslexic. He had heard of famous people being dyslexic, but it was helpful seeing an "ordinary person" accept her disability and become successful.

The following quote from Jack expresses his feelings about school experiences and being dyslexic. "Ever since I was diagnosed in second grade I have not been comfortable with being dyslexic. I was asked difficult questions by other students, to which I never gave a really truthful answer if I answered at all. It was worse for me because I was put in gifted classes. Knowing that I was like Albert Einstein, the super genius to end all super geniuses did help in some ways. However it never was enough to heal my wounds."

Despite his strong feelings about dyslexia, Jack did well in high school. He even looked forward to college because he loved learning. After visiting several schools, he chose West Virginia Wesleyan. He felt he could receive the help he needed without the stigma of being dyslexic. In fact, he said when he read the information about the college and that there was no stigma connected with having a disability, he sobbed. Jack visited Wesleyan and we had a very good interview. While he was at the college, Jack said he knew it was the right place for him. Jack enjoyed college and particularly appreciated Dr. Paul Richter, a chemistry professor, and Dr. Richter's wife, Margery Richter. He said Dr. Richter really prepared him for his future career. Mrs. Richter supervised the testing laboratory in the Learning Center. This was an accommodation that Jack felt he needed, and he appreciated Mrs. Richter's friendly attitude.

Jack was in the Lindamood-Bell ® reading program at the Learning Center. His major teacher in the program was Mike Brown. Mike "walked to a different drummer" and was able to reach students others could not. Jack said, "Mike Brown is the one who really taught me how to read. It took me fourteen years, but I finally learned." Jack now enjoys reading, but says he can read chemical journals easier than reading a children's book or *People Magazine.* (This is because we get out of the printed page what we bring to it. Jack brings a chemistry background to his reading.)

Another good experience for him was being a counselor in The Learning Center summer program for high school juniors. He particularly appreciated an evening at our home when he and the other student counselors were able to share their stories of growing up "dyslexic." In the week that followed many of the high school students talked with him about the similarities they had or were having in school. He said, "I felt I was really helping others!"

Not everything in college was enjoyable for Jack. He shared with me a difficult experience he had in the study skills class. Because I wanted the students to realize they were not alone with their dyslexia and other dyslexics found ways of coping, I assigned the book, *An Uncommon Gift.* This is the story of a young man who struggled with dyslexia, but later came to realize it was an "uncommon gift." The students were to compare the book to their own experiences. Jack found it stressful to read incidents similar to his own. This book made it necessary for him to recall his own experiences and remember his pain. Nevertheless, Jack recently thanked me for giving him the worst assignment he had in sixteen years! Today as he reflects on this book and the assignment, he has come to believe dyslexia really is an "uncommon gift."

Jack now believes dyslexia is a disadvantage in school but an advantage outside of school. He mentioned information from an article he had read in *The New York Times* which stated that 35% of entrepreneurs are dyslexic. He also stated that a couple of years ago in a commercial for Apple Computers entitled "*Think differently*" half of the people were dyslexic. He believes the reason for this may be that many dyslexics are "loaded" with imagination. He also thinks that for many, having dyslexia is like being members of an exclusive club of successful people. Jack said, "I view dyslexics as just another minority group, like racial and other minority groups in the world. The only difference is that dyslexics are invisible to the rest of the world because for the most part we do not have a distinguishable trait like skin color or have a different language as our first language." He also has discovered that in the work world people don't know he is dyslexic and really don't care. He usually keeps it a secret and it doesn't matter.

Since graduating from Wesleyan, Jack has had a successful career as a chemist. He currently works for US Steel in the Pittsburgh area where he lives. Jack still enjoys learning and is a member of an outstanding group, *The Society for Analytical Chemists*. At their meetings they give presentations and have discussions with outstanding chemists and professors from nearby universities.

Jack enjoys several activities. He appreciates walking, especially on primitive trails; cooking; and traveling. He has been in all fifty states. During one of his trips he visited some friends in Texas. One evening, he was particularly helped by Kathy, a young teacher. Kathy shared a story of a blind boy in her class who hadn't allowed his blindness to prevent him from becoming a geography champion even though he could not see a map. Jack then revealed to her his story of being dyslexic. It became an evening of soul searching which he will never forget.

Jack shared with me excerpts of an email he later sent to Kathy:

"... What you did, whether you know it or not, was to repair wounds I have carried around for the last twenty years. If I live to be a hundred it means I have carried around those wounds one out of every five days of my life. You don't know how grateful I am to you, Kathy. Ever since I was diagnosed in second grade, I have not been all that comfortable with being dyslexic. I was asked difficult questions by other students to which I never gave a truthful answer if I answered at all. It was worse for me because I was put in the gifted class as well.

Knowing that I was like Albert Einstein, the super genius to end all super geniuses did help in some ways . . . However it never was enough to heal my wounds. Since talking to you that night my handwriting has been different. It is so much neater and less chaotic . . . All I can say is "thank you!" I can't begin to tell you how much you have helped me; it is like having a weight removed from my back."

After struggling all his life with dyslexia, Jack now says people respond in disbelief when he tells them he is dyslexic. Now he can laugh if they accuse him of lying or not telling the truth about his "uncommon gift."

Jack has suggested insights and links to material which he believes will be helpful to others with learning disabilities.

1. Remember we have famous heroes like Edison, Picasso, Jay Leno, Erin Brockovich, Charles Schwab, Magic Johnson, John Lennon, George Westinghouse, Winston Churchill, and others who struggled with dyslexia.
2. Even though you have dyslexia, you have much in common with other people.
3. Remember you see the world differently from other people who don't have the "gift of dyslexia."
4. Heroes are great, but it is helpful to find "regular people" with dyslexia.
5. The following links may be helpful:
   a. http://www.dyslexia.com/famous.htm
      This is not a complete list but contains the names of many famous dyslexics.
   b. A link dealing with dyslexic entrepreneurs:
      http://www.nytimes.com/2007/12/06/business/06dyslexia.html?r=O
   c. Another interesting article in the New York Times is:
      http://www.nytimes.com/2013/04/28/opinion/sunday/diagnosing-the-wrong-deficit.html?pagewanted=all
   d. http://www.disability-marketing.com/profiles/fortune.php4

JOHN EDWARD CISZEK III

John Ciszek III is a graduatee of West Virginia Wesleyan College and is an outstanding business man. He was fortunate to grow up in a very supportive family. His mother, a lawyer, kept up on the research and opportunities for LD students. He is happily married and living in the Midwest.

John Ciszek's Story

John's parents noticed differences in him as a small child. He seemed to understand when adults were laughing at him and never really did the "cute" things that entertain adults. John was tested and diagnosed with Attention Deficit Disorder (ADD) when he was an 8 year old, after extreme learning and behavior difficulties surfaced in kindergarten through second grade. He always appeared very intelligent and seemed to learn quickly when information was presented verbally. He couldn't memorize the times tables or spelling words even though his parents drilled him repeatedly. His printing and handwriting were illegible and his desk and papers were always completely disorganized which drove all of his teachers crazy. John could never find his homework and always had a "story" to explain why he didn't do it. If he could produce the papers, they were ripped, dirty, and impossible to read. He didn't capitalize any words and seldom spelled words correctly. For example, he always spelled fire as "fier." When he was in first or second grade, John reversed letters, especially "d" and "b" but the school officials didn't find this important as "all children" reverse letters. At the private school he attended, neither the teachers nor principal could control John's behavior. When he refused to go to the principal's office, they would call the janitor to take him there. John was fearless and seemed never to be intimidated by the authority of principals, teachers, bullies, or his parents.

Due to his difficulties and labeling as "bad" at the private school, John transferred to the public school in third grade. His learning difficulties continued so he was tested at age 8. John was reading at the 1.5 year level, but had high level functioning in some areas at the 16.9 year level. When he was challenged, he paid attention and behaved well. However, when he already understood the material that other students were still working on, he had trouble staying in his seat and became mischievous. This was the time for fun which often meant trouble for him and others. He remembers trying to trip his kindergarten teacher – a prank she did not enjoy. On another occasion, he convinced the teacher and principal in his private school that he had fallen on the playground and was blind. They called his mother from work to pick him up, so he got out of school for the day. Since his mother knew his tricks, on the way to the doctor John reluctantly admitted that he could see. Looking back, John knows he must have been known as a trouble maker in elementary school. At about age 10, John got into trouble on the school bus and was told that he would be denied transportation to school for several days. Having arrived home that day before his parents, John decided to avoid problems from the school for a while. He disabled the family's telephone by putting scotch tape over the connecting wire end, replacing it into the jack, and going off to baseball practice. When his mother arrived home, the phone was dead and she spent hours trying to determine why the phone wouldn't work. Eventually John was discovered and suffered the consequences.

Although John was extremely bright, he was in both special education and the gifted program at his school. This created great social difficulties as his peers called him "retard," "stupid," and similar names. From a young age John was always extremely adept at "pushing the buttons" of both adults and his peers. He could anger the other children his age very easily with his verbal taunts.

John was always learning things from listening to adult conversation. On one occasion he remembers causally repeating the remarks a teacher made in class to an adult. As a result, the teacher was reprimanded and told to refrain from "discriminatory" behavior. At age 10, John went to the ceremony where his mother was admitted to practice before the United States Supreme Court. He sat spellbound as the Chief Justice read a decision on a case from Virginia issued by the Court relating to the "privileges and immunities" clause in the U.S. Constitution. Afterwards, he began asking his mother questions and she was shocked at his understanding of the facts and the law. (Actually, his mother says she knew little about this kind of constitutional question and didn't know how to respond to John's questions.)

Although John's parents struggled to determine the best way to handle his mischievous conduct and social/school problems, they were wise in handling them. They were able to discipline and teach him while enabling him to maintain his self-esteem. John says maybe it was because his parents didn't always use the top down "parent to child" approach. He thinks his dad actually enjoyed some of his antics. His mother was always ready to take on any authority figure, including teachers, police, neighbors, or bullies if she felt John was not in the wrong. His parents also seemed to understand how John felt when he wanted to be driven to school instead of sitting on the bus. John remembers his mother saying that when she was in school she wanted to drive to school too because she hated the people on the bus. At times, John says his parents actually seemed different because they appeared to side with him against other adults or authority figures. Yet, John's parents always maintained that line which was not to be crossed and John knew where it was. So somehow, they got through all of his school and interpersonal problems even though it was often a very rocky road to travel.

When John was in eighth grade his parents bought him a laptop computer and fought to get the school to accept John's homework and other papers prepared electronically. This was before computers were generally in use and he felt self-conscious using it. The computer was not compatible with the Apple computers used by the school in that era and there was always a problem trying to print out his work while in school. Most of the teachers would look at John's work on the computer and give him credit without the need for hard copies. However, one teacher believed John was using the computer because he was lazy and a faker. This was back in the days when there were teachers who not only did not understand learning disabilities but also were not convinced they existed. The computer really helped John to write papers, especially by correcting spelling mistakes which were a big problem for him. Unfortunately, someone decided to steal the computer which was worth about $2,000 at the time. John felt the school was unfair when this happened because the school personnel seemed focused on his failure to keep the computer in a safe place, rather than being focused on the person who committed the theft.

Another problem John remembers was taking tests that used a separate answer sheet on which you fill in a box to indicate the correct answer. He sometimes knew the right answer but put it on the wrong line. He developed a coping strategy for this problem by writing the letter of the correct box on the question sheet as well as filling in the answer sheet. He could then check and correct the answer sheet if necessary. His parents also fought for him to be permitted to take the untimed SAT test for college entrance evaluation.

Students with learning disabilities universally have had to deal with being put down by people who do not understand. John remembers one such incident while he was in high school. He was looking at a college catalog in the library when one of his teachers came to him and said, "What are you looking at that for? You are not going to college." As John looks back at that experience, he sees it as part of the motivation which helped him go to college and succeed. He would show him! John is sure this teacher would have been surprised if he read the article in the *Wall Street Journal* which listed John among those receiving Masters degrees from Wake Forest University after traveling and observing in China as part of their degree program.

For parents of an ADD, ADHD or any LD child, it can be very difficult to define the parameters of the parent/child relationship. This can also be a problem in the teacher/student relationship. Many times, as a young child, John inserted himself into what was perceived as "adult business." His mother believes that he felt himself on equal footing with parents and teachers intellectually so he was not intimidated into keeping his thoughts to himself. John's high level executive functioning and abstract reasoning were always well above average for his chronological age. His mother remembers when he was about five years old, he was with his father outside by the shed watching his dad install a "bug zapper" with an electric eye. The equipment was supposed to turn on when the electric eye sensed darkness. His dad was thinking and trying to figure out the best way to install the eye and John talked incessantly, expressing his ideas on the subject. Finally, his father just yelled for him to be quiet because he couldn't think. In the end, John's suggestions for installing the eye were correct and his father had to recognize his five-year-old's ability to contribute to adult problem solving.

On another occasion, J.'s mother had damaged the family car when she ran over rocks that had fallen from a hillside onto the public road. The repairs were very costly and John felt free to contribute to the conversation that perhaps the property owner should be liable for the damage. John thought the owner "should have known" about damage that could occur when rocks from his hillside fell into the public thoroughfare. Of course, this was infuriating to his mother who was a lawyer and had not thought of this alternative at all. There are many other occasions where John's conduct and problem solving ability did not ingratiate him with the teachers and other grownups who felt that a child should not be included in "adult issues." As a result, John was either greatly liked or disliked by adults with whom he had contact and there was no middle ground. The consequences to John were that he could easily become resentful when he was disciplined or put in his "proper place" as a child for speaking out of turn or being disrespectful.

John's parents believed in him and encouraged him to attend college. His mother did research on learning disabilities and college programs for students with learning disabilities. She encouraged him to attend West Virginia Wesleyan and its Special Service Program. It was a good match for him.

At Wesleyan John knew that accounting courses were difficult so he waited until his sophomore year to take Accounting I. But by the time he graduated he had become an accounting major. Mike Ervin, his favorite accounting professor, encouraged him. He remembers Dr.

Ervin coming up to him and shaking his hand privately after a test, telling him that he was proud of his grade on the test, which had topped the best student in the class. That type of encouragement later helped John decide to tackle a master's program at Wake Forest.

After graduating from Wesleyan, John attempted to take the CPA exam. This was very difficult for him because all of the old problems with recording answers on standardized tests caused him difficulties. John became very frustrated when he missed passing this exam several times by one or two points. John decided to move on as he really wasn't eager to spend a career in public accounting or doing people's taxes every year. Having spent about three years in public accounting, John moved on to private industry and held several financial positions in large corporations. John was awarded his MBA from Wake Forest with a concentration in International Business. This concentration has been valuable to him as he has made various trips to China. He said, "The officials at Wake Forest claimed I was the first person to come through their executive MBA program who had an official diagnosed learning disability. They put accommodations in place, but I never had to use them." However, that is not to say that the MBA program was easy or without difficulties. Sometimes John had to struggle to handle his job, school, and family responsibilities. There were many ups and downs during the two year program, but with determination and the support of his wife, he was successful.

For two years John worked as the Manager of Financial Planning and Analysis for a Fortune 500 Corporation with a focus in the fire and security division. He especially enjoyed his work and in reflecting about it, John said, "I wonder how many accountants with ADHD, LD, and dyslexia are responsible for the international financial planning and strategy for a seven billion dollar business segment in one of the largest corporations on earth!" He added, "I owe most of my success to my parents who did not allow me to be passed over or pushed into alternate programs instead of the academic courses in high school. They made my education a priority to the point of paying extra fees to the Learning Center to help insure my success. I owe Wesleyan's Learning Center big time as well."

John was always looking to advance in his career. After about one year in fire and security, he found an opening that he thought would be an excellent expansion into other fields. This was a position that required growth in his skills in an area not really related to accounting or financial analysis. The move was to another large corporation which looked very good "on paper." The realities of the position were quite different from what John anticipated. He was expected to perform financial analysis as well as cost analysis with very little support in retrieving data that he needed to do his job. Management required their executive employees to keep detailed notes that were inspected regularly. his old problems from high school resurfaced. His personal notes weren't legible, the pages were ripped out and sometimes lost, and he had to scan and copy most of his own documents that were needed in his job. This was overwhelming and John began to suffer from stress and chronic worrying. The stress also caused physical problems that added to the overload. John tried working all hours of the day and night because he had never given up before or let himself be beaten by the "system." But this time, John was not a young teenager in school; he was a maturing adult, and eventually John recognized that he could not continue the pace without serious repercussions in both his personal and professional life. John left this job and had to take a "time out" to catch his breath.

John's "time out" did not last long. Within a month he found a new and better position as North American Pricing Manger with Mettler Toledo. He is responsible for all pricing structure, rules and implementation, and has taught over 550 employees about the company's pricing and strategies.

His mother believes that John will say that he feels he has been very lucky in securing appropriate employment; but the facts show that hard work may be more important than luck. He works harder than most other employees and he is dedicated to succeeding in any job he undertakes. His new position was almost the "perfect" fit for his interests. But nothing is perfect as we all know! John had to move to another state and deal with the problems everyone faces when trying to sell their home. His wife had to give up her job and search for employment in their new city. This upheaval caused stress, but it was not nearly as bad as the atmosphere that John left behind. He loves his work now in an area of focus that requires him to learn new things all of the time. His natural resilience is helping him to feel successful again. He says that it was his family who helped him to pull through. His mother supported him and his wife stayed by his side as she has done for many years. His mother remembers a family member talking to him on the night of his high school graduation party. His cousin said, "You will be as much as your family is willing to invest in you." He never forgot this and says he is very lucky that he has a family willing to "invest in him" all the way.

John knows that the real world offers many challenges especially in the work place. It is very difficult to know how or when to discuss something (like your learning difference) with your boss and explain the type of changes an employer can make to help you do your job better. There is always fear that someone who doesn't understand will conclude that you are stupid (like some teachers twenty years ago) or not a good fit for the organization. (The author agrees with John on this point, but feels that it usually is important to have this discussion, in spite of the difficulty.)

John's experiences in the business world and his time out experience have led him to a new venture. In order to always have something to fall back on to support his family, he has begun his own company, JC Enterprises. This is a federally-licensed firearms manufacturer and arms dealer which designs and manufactures firearms for police, law enforcement, the military, and the average citizen.

John has good insight to share with young people struggling to overcome learning disabilities and ADD or ADHD. John said he realized before starting college that he could choose not to take medication and be a failure; or he could accept medication and be successful, living a full and productive life. He added, "Unfortunately, to this day I still have to take ADHD meds, I am dead in the water without them."

John went on to say that it is important to assure an LD child or youth that he/she is smart, maybe even smarter than the kids who are calling him/her stupid. "There are different ways of being smart. Filling in the wrong box on an answer sheet does not mean you are dumb." He added, "I think the biggest pitfall for students entering college is the belief that they cannot make it…they will. I am living proof."

BRYAN BAKER

Bryan Baker, "Mr. Missions", is positive he has been called by God into Christian ministry. This calling has taken him to several countries. Through his faith in God, hard work, advocacy, and the support of persons such as his parents, he is succeeding in ministry and in life. His story is also a journey of growing from hiding his learning disability because of the stigma he felt, to accepting its positive as well as negative aspects and celebrating the fact he has learned to cope. His story is an inspiration to others.

Bryan's Story

Bryan was an enthusiastic elementary school student who had lots of friends and was liked by his teachers. However, Bryan and his mother realized he had a problem. He was very good in math and science but frustrated because he was in the lowest reading group. His mother, who was an educator, felt there was something wrong. He was on the 99th percentile in the Math and Science sections of the standardized test but average in reading. His teachers were not alarmed at this because they thought he was an average reader; but his parents continued to be troubled. By 6th grade they decided to have him tested at West Virginia University. This testing showed he did have a reading problem related to long and short term memory and memory transference. He was eligible for some special education classes, but he didn't want to be placed in special classes because there was a stigma attached to learning disabled (LD) placement. The attitude of many was that these were the "dumb" kids. Bryan, like many LD students, preferred to deny his need for special help and thus avoid the stigma that was attached to it.

As a teenager he struggled with self-identity and spirituality. He asked probing questions, striving to learn all he could about God. Early in his high school career he took American History and Native American History. The teacher for both courses was Mr. Ryan who, Bryan said, "changed my life." In these classes, he learned and was fascinated by the diverse religions and spirituality of the American Indians. As a result he began to explore his own faith in search of such rich spirituality. As he did, his relationship with God was strengthened and he began to feel God was calling him into ministry. However, he didn't want to be a "stuffy old preacher" or pastor. It was better to ignore this call. During the summer at a Youth Celebration for high school students at West Virginia Wesleyan College, he finally acknowledged and said yes to God's call, but he didn't know where it would lead.

In high school he was very involved in many activities which included playing football and wrestling. He also was taking a heavy academic load, was working on his Eagle Scout badge, and busy with many church and school activities. He was trying to burn the candle at both ends and please everyone, especially his mother and dad. His dad who had been a colonel in the army had high standards for his son: Bryan was never to be a quitter in anything and should be the best in everything he did or in every organization he joined.

During his senior year in high school Bryan realized his next educational step was college. When the President of West Virginia Wesleyan spoke at his church, Bryan talked with him afterwards. Bryan was interested in Wesleyan, but following the conversation he feared he could never keep up with college assignments. He told his mother he wouldn't go to college, but become a trash collector.

The pressure he felt and his feelings of inadequacy caused him to reach a point of desperation at times and even to think of suicide. Finally he became so depressed and physically ill that he had to be hospitalized. His mother was very supportive at this time and The Rev. Dr. Keith

Reider, a pastoral counselor, was very helpful. The hospitalization became a time of reflection for him. He knew he enjoyed the Honors English class and he belonged there; but reading aloud before the entire class was a stressful and embarrassing time for him. Previously he had not been able to admit that his earlier diagnosis of a learning disability was true. Now he realized his reading was a major problem. In addition to his difficulty in reading aloud, he could not read fast enough to finish his work, even though his comprehension was fine. Because he understood material so well other students would ask him for help. He would tutor them and they would finish their work in school; but he had to carry books home and spend hours on his homework, working until 1 or 2 o'clock in the morning. When he took the PSAT, he was sure he would not get into West Virginia University because his test scores were very low; therefore he never applied. He believed his low scores were the result of his not completing enough of the test. Now he recognized his problem. This realization made him swallow his pride and be tested again for a learning disability.

As a result of being positively diagnosed with a reading problem and Attention Deficit Disorder (ADD), he was able to take the ACT untimed. This made a tremendous difference. After the untimed testing he was offered a scholarship to the University without even applying. He applied instead to West Virginia Wesleyan College and was offered the Presidential Scholarship which was one of Wesleyan's best. He also was given an opportunity to work in the Bonner Program (a service scholarship opportunity). Additionally, he was accepted in both the Honors Program and the Special Service Program (LD program). Being accepted into the Special Service Program was also an honor since not all who applied were accepted.

I had the privilege to begin working with Bryan during his freshman year. He was in a Reading and Study Skills Course and a Christian Education class: "Introduction to Church and Service Vocations." In the reading and study skills class, I was able to help him by emphasizing, "It is not the hours you put in, but what you put in the hours." This was helpful advice for him. In analyzing his reading problem, I realized that although he understood material, he had a type of comprehension problem which was due to his slow reading. He was a word by word reader which is okay for short sentences, but not college work. Since the short term memory can only hold seven items, by the time he got to the end of a sentence he had forgotten the first part, making it necessary to reread the material. We worked on a speed reading program where he learned to see an "eyeful of words", thus shortening the number of items per sentence for the short term memory. His reading improved greatly and he quadrupled his speed.

His increased speed and coping strategies allowed him to do well in college. He said for most classes, he continued to use a technique he had learned earlier. He "studied the professor", which meant he listened intently looking at the face of the professor and trying to understand his point of view. He had a note taker from the Learning Center, and reworked her notes as a method of reviewing. He had a study partner who read the text, and they could share together. The method worked for him not only at Wesleyan but also in graduate school.

Although Bryan had many positive experiences both in and out of the class room; he had his ups and downs also. He had to accept that a learning disability is always with you and you always have to cope and face challenges. It was frustrating for him to share with his professors about his disability and take exams in the Learning Center. He felt he had to study harder than most students and couldn't enjoy "over the hump night", a night when others partied.

During the spring semester of his freshman year, he had physical problems which resulted in hospitalization. After taking tests, the doctors realized the ADD medicine wasn't working and they needed to change the prescription. While in the hospital he appreciated the support of students and faculty members who were encouraging him to return to class. Bryan and his mother recall how difficult it was for him to miss so many classes and be prepared for exams.

When he returned to class, the new medicines he was now taking created another problem. He had to fight falling asleep in class, becoming embarrassed when his efforts didn't succeed. He really did want to learn as he enjoyed his classes and professors, but he felt his friends and professors didn't realize this. Although he recognized that he had an LD problem, he still didn't want to share this with others. He was in the stage of recognizing the problem but not really accepting it. Finally, he found it necessary to discuss these problems with me, and he was able to accept that he learned differently from others, and we were able to develop new coping strategies.

There were many people that impacted his life at this time. Bryan wanted me to mention a few. He began as both a Biology and Psychology major. Dr. Richard Calef, chair of the psychology department, appreciated Bryan's discussions in class and encouraged him to think about getting a PhD in psychology, even though Bryan was only a freshman. He also recommended him as a tutor for the class. This meant working harder. I challenged him in Christian Education to listen to ways God was calling him to ministry. He said this was helpful because he still didn't want to be a pastor or preacher, but kept feeling God's call. Dr. Herbert Coston, history professor, gave him an independent study on South Africa, challenging him to read and seek to understand the culture where he was going to study during a semester abroad. Dr. Kathy Gregg and Dr. Carl Colson, biology professors, led a January term course to Belize which opened his eyes about needs in underdeveloped countries, reinforcing his realization God was calling him to be a missionary. Mr. Doug Duffield, the assistant director of the Parish House, which is a United Methodist mission project in West Virginia, worked with him as a friend and mentor. Working with Doug helped him balance academics with his love for service. He said he enjoyed going to class with a tool belt on one shoulder and a back pack full of books on the other. Bryan said Doug really enriched his life. He also enjoyed a college work scholarship, working in the Learning Center. Work, service, and study seemed to help him keep his balance. Another person who influenced him was the Reverend Ron McCauley who has helped him as a friend and pastor.

As part of the requirements of a Christian Education major, Bryan had to have an internship. We talked about an internship where he could use his kinesthetic learning style, his interest in various cultures, and missionary opportunities. He found the perfect one for himself: working a summer with the Ute Mountain Indian tribe in White Mesa, Utah.

Another wonderful experience was his senior semester abroad where he studied at the University of Stellenbosch in South Africa. Following the semester he had an amazing summer traveling and living with African friends.

After returning home, tragedy struck. He was hospitalized and almost died. The doctors were puzzled and were ready to give up. His mother thought that he must have caught malaria in Africa, but the doctors diagnosed it as a stomach virus. Because he continued getting worse, his parents took him to a hospital where malaria was finally diagnosed. Thanks to his mother and the doctors, Bryan recovered. When he was ill, he had time to continue discerning his call to ministry. Bryan said, "I knew I would live because I had not finished the work God intended me to complete." His discernment led him to feel he was called to be a deacon, an ordained minister who often serves God beyond the local church.

After recovering, Bryan accepted a position to work with troubled teens as a teacher/counselor at a wilderness camp for juvenile delinquents. It was challenging, but he still felt this was not where God was calling him. He wanted to return to Africa as a missionary. An opportunity came to serve in missions, but not overseas. A "10-10-10 program" sponsored by the United Methodist Board of Global Ministry was to begin in Huntington, WV, and a director was needed. After prayer, Bryan knew God was calling him to this mission, and he was hired as the director.

Bryan shared with me: "Though my heart remained focused on mission to distant lands, I was presented the challenge of starting a mission project from scratch in a greatly impoverished area of the city of Huntington. I lived and worked in the midst of racially and economically segregated communities. I served as a link between these different worlds. I chose to live in the 'hood' and devote myself to the communities." In three years, Hope Ministries of East Huntington grew to involve home repair, disaster relief, a food pantry, a Tae Kwon Do School, homeless ministries, and home Bible studies in housing projects. The summer work camp program grew so much that it would have been impossible to carry out without the help of an AmeriCorps staff person.

As director of the program Brian was called to speak and preach at several churches. He met many ministers who became outstanding mentors. These experiences made him begin to question his call to be a deacon. Was he called to be an elder (an ordained preacher/pastor)?

He knew he wanted to be a missionary and began thinking possibly it would be better to go to the mission field as an elder so he could offer the sacraments and maybe even serve a small church.

The call to the ministry of an elder became stronger. As his three-year appointment as a 10-10-10 missionary drew to a close, Bryan realized it was time to go to seminary. He became interested in Duke Divinity School, but his fears of his LD and physical problems gave him doubts. Even though he had been successful at Wesleyan, he was a typical LD—questioning his own ability. His mother also had some fears and thought possibly a smaller seminary closer to home would be good. He liked Wesley Seminary and the challenging opportunities for service in the Washington, DC, area.

Despite his fear and his real interest in Wesley Seminary, he felt God was calling him to Duke. He responded to this call and began studies at Duke Divinity School. Duke was the right place for Bryan. He matured academically and spiritually and had opportunity for missions, his love. He became a trail blazer in going and opening opportunities for others to experience mission trips. He was able to be part of three mission trips. As a kinesthetic learner, mission trips were ideal for Bryan; but more than his learning style it was his "missionary's heart" that made these experiences life changing.

In 2005 Bryan joined faculty and other students on trips to Rwanda and Uganda. He calls these trips his "Pilgrimage of Pain and Hope", and describes his pain in the following story:

> "In April of 1994, the Hutu majority population of Rwanda set out to completely exterminate the Tutsis, the ethnic minority. I met young people who were part of this genocide. Friend killed friend. One young man in a shower of tears told about killing his girlfriend. Now he could not even understand why. One of my most painful experiences was a visit to a memorial site where an elementary school once stood. The classrooms were filled with skeletal remains of children and teachers. As I was walking amongst the bodies, I walked into a protruding foot. I staggered back; a rush of fear entered my body. I had made contact. It somehow

became more personal as I looked at this child. It was not a pile of bones, but a child whose body was wrenched with pain, frozen in his last moment of agony. My heart was still pounding as I stepped outside for a breath of fresh air and a handful of stinging tears. I then attempted to pray, but I could not find the words."

His experiences in Uganda were not as painful as in Rwanda. As part of his field placement he spent the entire summer in Uganda, teaching in both an elementary and secondary school, and "shadowing" the priest and helping him with pastoral duties and prayer. Bryan also had the opportunity to go to the war zone in the North, visiting refugee camps and also learning about child soldiers.

Bryan loved teaching, but was very bothered by the poverty. Some children had nothing; only a few had papers, pens, and books. Many teachers shared their books with the pupils. When Bryan shared this situation with his mother, a deacon at First United Methodist Church in Clarksburg, West Virginia, the church supplied sports equipment. The children and youth loved learning and playing games. Bryan knows he learned far more than he taught and will never forget the experience.

The trip to the war zone in North Uganda was another painful experience. He shared with me stories of the "night commuters", children who live in fear of being abducted from their homes. They hike up to two miles every night to sleep in the protected walls of hospitals and churches with armed guards. It is necessary to leave home because rebels slip into the villages undetected in the night and take young boys and girls, forcing them to fight and kill. If they refuse they are tortured, mutilated, and often killed. These child soldiers may be as young as six years old.

Bryan returned to Duke a changed person, and realized his need to go back to the mission field. In March of 2006 Bryan was able to go on another mission trip sponsored by both Duke Divinity School and Duke Medical School. He not only experienced another culture but also visited hospitals and an orphanage, thus gaining a deeper awareness of the pastoral role in healing. As a result he said that he now has a better understanding of life and death, and a pastor's opportunities.

When sharing his hospital experience, he said he became especially close to three children. Lona was a little girl with whom he colored pictures. By visiting several times he saw her blossom and finally able to go home. Another was a little boy who enjoyed Bryan's stories of playing soccer, and who told Bryan that he played soccer and was faster than anyone else. He especially liked Bryan to read to him over and over again. The third child was Jeff, a 12 year-old who looked half his age and was dying from AIDS. He was an orphan whose mother had already died from AIDS. Although Jeff was too weak to hold crayons and draw, he loved to have Bryan drawing for him and telling him stories. Bryan loved visiting him. These experiences helped Bryan realize he will always want to have a ministry with children. It was a joy seeing some get well, but difficult for him when he returned to the US to hear that Jeff had died.

The greatest event for Bryan at Duke was meeting Jaya, who became his wife. He and Jaya were both in line for tickets for Duke's basketball games. Jaya heard Bryan talk about missions and became interested in the conversation. Her parents were from India and she was aware of the mission work there. The wait was long and they talked and talked. While there, Jaya lost her cell phone which was an event that changed their lives. Bryan had enjoyed meeting Jaya, but had no idea how to see her again. As luck or God would have it, he found her cell phone and returned it to her. This brought them together. Much of their courtship was long distance because Bryan graduated and began serving a church in West Virginia, while she was completing her studies at Duke, becoming a Doctor of Physical Therapy.

Bryan appreciated his professors and his opportunities for studying and learning at Duke. His physical and learning problems presented challenges; but his motivation, prayer, and God's help allowed him to graduate with a Master of Divinity Degree. At graduation he was honored with a special award for his leadership in developing and leading mission opportunities. He was known as "Mr. Missions". After graduation and commissioning as a Provisional Elder, he was appointed to Claypool United Methodist Church in Davin, WV, an area known for much poverty and drug abuse, making it a mission field in itself.

On July 4th 2009, Bryan and Jaya were married in the lovely Duke gardens. I was privileged to be one of the officiating ministers. It was a beautiful day. They are a wonderful couple, both called by God to serve. Bryan was ordained an Elder in June 2010 and continues to serve as a United Methodist pastor in Churches in West Virginia. Jaya is a doctor of Physical Therapy in a local hospital and also busy as a full time mom. They are proud parents of Elijah Zachery who was born in 2012.

Their story is only beginning. Bryan will never grow out of his learning disabilities, but God has given him the ability to cope and a wonderful wife to help him. He hopes to return to the mission field someday with Jaya by his side.

Bryan closed our last interview by saying, "My road to ministry has been anything but ordinary. I have seen God work in many strange and wonderful ways throughout the course of my life. I do not know where life will take me, but I know that I will not make a move without God's approval. I have promised God a life of servanthood, and the rest is in His hands."

Bryan with children from Uganda.

KELLY POLLARD PAXTON

Kelly says, "There is no way I could have succeeded without my Mom and Dad." That is a recurring theme in this book and Kelly is one of many who say this gratefully. A 2000 graduate of West Virginia Wesleyan College, Kelly is a wife and mother of 3 and a successful Special Education teacher and Special Ed Coordinator in Roanoke County, Virginia.

Kelly's Story

Kelly's dream was to be a Special Education teacher. This dream became a reality! She has been with the Roanoke County Public School System for 10 years. She began as an elementary Special Education teacher and still continues to teach; but her talents were recognized and in addition to teaching, she is the Special Education Coordinator in her school. In this role, Kelly reviews the compliance laws and the school's policies. She supervises and mentors other Special Education teachers, reviews IEP's (Individualized Education Program), has meetings with parents and students, determines eligibility for special programs, and provides guidance to regular teachers and counselors. She really cares and helps parents, students, and other teachers succeed.

As a Special Education Coordinator her role extends beyond her school. She meets at the central office once a month with the Director of the Roanoke County Schools and other coordinators. The director goes over the new changes for the county, and Kelly takes the information back to her school. She explains the changes and gives her teachers any special training needed.

Kelly's dream became a reality because of hard work, determination, support from family and others, as well as advocacy from parents and herself. Kelly's learning disability, involving both auditory processing and reading comprehension, was discovered in second grade. Today she works with second graders with learning disabilities and understands them.

When she began to have problems in school, her parents had her tested by Gene Watson, a well-known psychologist in Roanoke. Dr. Watson was a popular speaker, known by members of the Learning Disability Association and the Orton Dyslexia Society. Dr. Watson told Kelly's mother that LD children were like turtles: they liked to stay in their hard shell and be sure of themselves before they would stick their head out of the shell. Dr. Watson inspired Kelly's mom and made her believe that if she had to, she could "take on the school system".

After her experience with Dr. Watson, Mrs. Pollard agreed to have the school test Kelly. Kelly hated the testing because she felt she had to do "stupid things". She disliked Mr. Barber, the psychologist who tested her; she blamed him for being put in the Special Ed classes which she hated because classmates taunted her and called her stupid. Later in life when they worked together as colleagues, she appreciated him. His wife was her favorite teacher! After becoming a teacher, it was a privilege to work with her as a colleague and friend.

Although she hated to go to the "Sped class" in elementary school, she loved her teacher, Sheila Barber. She was a very caring person. She helped her learn to read and also helped with special problems. For instance, there was a classmate who made fun of her. Mrs. Barber took care of him!!! (In high school this classmate discovered he had Attention Deficit Hyperactive Disorder, and became a good friend of Kelly.)

When Mrs. Barber realized that Kelly was upset being called learning disabled, she called her mother and suggested she use the term learning difference. Kelly's mother talked to her about how some people need to wear glasses to learn. Others need hearing aids. This clicked with Kelly, and she felt better about herself.

One of the most helpful experiences Mrs. Barber did for Kelly and other special ed kids was to write a play about famous people with learning disabilities which included Tom Cruise, Albert Einstein, Cher, and others. The Special Ed students presented it to the whole school. Kelly felt more accepted after that. Mrs. Barber really planted the seed for Kelly to aspire to be a special education teacher.

Kelly remembers her middle school teachers. She had both painful and good experiences. It was no problem to go to the "sped class" because everyone changed classes. One of her painful experiences was with a math teacher. The teacher did not believe in learning disabilities, and she would not allow Kelly to use a multiplication chart when taking tests. The use of the multiplication chart was part of her IEP (Individualized Education Program). Kelly's mother immediately requested an IEP meeting. It was there she became the "assertive advocate". She remembers shaking her finger at the teacher and saying, "I know the law. The IEP is a legal document that you are bound by law to follow and if you don't I will sue your pants off." Now Kelley supervises others and tries to prevent students in her school from having embarrassing and frustrating experiences like this.

By ninth grade Kelly was fully mainstreamed and felt good about herself. However, another obstacle had to be faced. An algebra teacher told her she could not take Algebra 2 and she should not go to college. Kelly was devastated! She had to go to college to fulfill her dream of being a Special Education teacher. Without the family knowing it, the teacher had Kelly take a vocational test. The teacher told her that according to the tests, she would be a good dog groomer or hair dresser. Kelly cried and was crushed because these careers were not her dream.

Again her mother became an assertive advocate. She said to the teacher, "How dare you test my child without our permission? She will go to college even if I have to go along. My child will not be a failure."

These were not idle words. When Kelly had problems with reading and comprehending a special book in a short amount of time for a college class, Mrs. Pollard drove to Wesleyan and rented a room at a motel. There she and Kelly spent the weekend reading and discussing the book together. This resulted in Kelly passing her exam.

Before Kelly applied to Wesleyan, her parents made her go to a special summer program at Wesleyan which was designed for LD high school students between their junior and senior year. She did not want to attend. She wanted to stay home to be near her boyfriend. Although she fought with her parents about going, she had a different attitude after she was there. She loved it and appreciated the college students who were members of the Special Support Program who were assisting in the program. She was also thrilled with the opportunity to take a regular college course for credit, to prove she could do it. When the summer was over, she was enthusiastic about her experience and applied for early acceptance to Wesleyan.

She loved Wesleyan and especially the staff and students in the Special Support Program; but she was disappointed that Buckhannon was a small town. She went to Marshall University for a weekend thinking she might want to transfer. After the weekend, she knew that she needed the small college atmosphere and Wesleyan's Special Support Program. In addition to the Learning Center, she loved the small classes and the "caring professors".

In her reflections about the Learning Center, she felt the tutors, note takers, and the Lindamood-Bell ® program were very helpful. She especially appreciated having the opportunity to work in the Center as a student assistant. In her junior and senior years she was given the responsibility to open the Center on Saturday and Sunday evenings and to be available to help other students. A special thrill for her was to be an assistant in the Summer Program where she had first been a student. She got to help high school juniors the way Amy Shearman (See her story) and other caring staff of the Learning Center had helped her. The professionals in the Learning Center were models for her future career.

In addition to the Learning Center staff, she appreciated many of her professors who went beyond the call of duty to help. She felt the opportunity that Dr. Herbert Coston gave to all his students to take individual oral exams was great. It was an opportunity not just for LD students but for any student so she didn't feel different. She enjoyed the privileges given by professors for individual work in their offices and for socials events in their homes. She remembers an experience during her senior year. Dr. Fortney, her major professor, helped her in the office, and opened her home to small groups having similar problems, to study and discuss together.

She was so glad she had chosen to remain at a small caring school. She also repeated that there is no way she could have succeeded without her Mom and Dad.

KELLY'S ADVICE TO LD STUDENTS:

1. The word, "<u>can't</u>", should not be in your vocabulary.
2. Never give up.
3. Dream big and go for it.
4. Strive to do the best you can.
5. Advocate for yourself. Find out the accommodations you need.
6. You and your parents need to be honest about having an LD. It is nothing to be ashamed of.

KARIM BADWAN

Karim has had an outstanding career in theater, film, opera, and television. His career has taken him all over the United States and in many other parts of the world. He has also taught at his Alma Mater, West Virginia Wesleyan College.

Karim's Story

Karim began school in the early 1980's, and found it an unpleasant experience. He wasn't able to pay attention in first and second grades and was easily distracted, which was a problem for him and his teachers. His mother, a nurse, was very perceptive and insisted that the school have him tested. From the diagnosis, it was determined that he was ADD (Attention Deficit Disorder.) At that time few people had heard of ADD. He was fortunate to have an outstanding doctor who prescribed both medication and coping devices. Karim feels that in the beginning the diagnosis of his disability "was a disability within a disability." He was going through a rough time at home because his parents were getting a divorce, and he used his disability as an excuse for not doing his school work.

In eighth grade he went to Marblewood, a boarding school. Here his attitude changed. He remembers four outstanding teachers: Dryden Clark, Glen Sanchez, Richard Chamberlain, and Hugh Chaining. They changed his life! These teachers helped him see he should be more than a "jock." He should be a good student. They were excellent advisors.

During Karim's first year in high school Dryden Clark was his advisor. He was an amazing man. He had been in the military, and an all American lacrosse player. Just before Karim began high school Dryden had a stroke. He lost the use of half of his body. Karim said, "I remember one night sitting in the study hall complaining, and Dryden Clark told me, 'you can let your disability cripple you and you will never go anywhere or you can move on seeing it as a difference not a disability and choose to succeed.'" Karim never forgot these words. He says he believes: "Everyone has some kind of stigma and you choose to fail or succeed."

While in high school, Karim had another choice to make. Because of his Attention Deficit Disorder difficulties, he had trouble paying attention in class and also focusing to get work done. His therapist prescribed Ritalin for him and told him, "you have two choices to cope with your disability: Take your medicine or learn coping skills." In high school Karim chose to take his medicine but decided in college to use coping skills.

Karim appreciated Marblewood high school. He felt he was ready for college in several ways. The school had prepared him for living away from home, meeting academic challenges, and accepting responsibility. In high school Karim played four sports: hockey, lacrosse, skiing, and soccer. When he got to college, he was willing to follow his mother's advice and concentrate on his studies rather than becoming a campus athlete. However he did participate in a lacrosse club.

Karim loved history classes and entered Wesleyan intending to be a history major and to also take many philosophy courses. I asked him how he became involved in theatre. He said his interest and later his career began when some students asked him to go with them for the tryouts for one act plays. After trying out, he received a part in a play. He was hooked! This was the first of many acting opportunities. Actors, crew members, and faculty worked together producing shows. They became like family. Theatre became a big part of his life.

Karim found himself very busy trying to be a good student and participating in dramatics. Because of his tight schedule, he really valued the Learning Center since it provided the freedom to use the accommodations that were important to him. He particularly appreciated staff members who would give him advice when needed, but encouraged him to figure things out for himself. The tips he received helped him enhance his ability to focus, which is needed for both acting and studying.

While at Wesleyan an opportunity came for him to attend the South Eastern Theatre Conference with members of the Theatre Department. He said he really felt terrified standing with over a hundred students to try out for parts in the play. Finally he said to himself, "I can't do this." He appreciated that one of his professors, Tomry Lathum, stepped in to advise him to take this opportunity at the conference to learn about lighting and other technical areas essential to play production. He followed this advice and that experience inspired him to begin thinking of the importance of the technical aspect of the theatre.

After returning from the conference, Karim focused his attention on the technical side of theatre productions. Tomry Lathum, the technical director in the Drama Department, appreciated Karim's skills in lighting and gave him opportunities to use his talents. Since Karim was working his way through college as an electrician, he was very knowledgeable in planning the lights for the productions. As he worked on the many facets of the theatre, his love for theatre grew. He was able to combine the knowledge he had gained in history, philosophy, physics, art, and other subjects with his work in theatre. When he graduated from Wesleyan, he knew his future career would be in the theatre.

After graduating from Wesleyan, he again went to the South Eastern Theatre Conference. While there, he applied for technical positions. His first position was with the Santa Fe Opera Company. He began as an apprentice and in his second year became a staff electrician. This company was known as the "boot camp" for theatre positions. Some of the best designers and technicians in the country were there. It was a wonderful place to start his career and to learn even more about the theatre. He also made many friends from conservatories, universities, and other colleges.

After working at the Opera Company for two years, one of his friends invited Karim to work with him at the Arkansas Reparatory

Theatre in Little Rock, Arkansas, as a master technician. He was pleased with this opportunity, but continued to have a goal for himself to be a designer. Art had always been important in his life, and a career in design would allow him to be a part of this field he loved. He hoped someday a chance would come for him to become a designer.

After a year at the Reparatory Theatre, he was offered a job as a designer for the opera. He worked at the opera for a year and decided it was time to return to Boston. However, the opera manager called urging him to come back as the master electrician. They needed him. He agreed to return with the stipulation that he would be able to design two shows.

His first show to design was *W; t* (pronounced Wit) which is about a female English professor who has ovarian cancer. (As Professor Badwan at Wesleyan, he read this play each year to the Wesleyan nursing students.) The second show was a world premiere, *Left Hand Singing*. This play is about the civil rights movement and the kids that got lost when they went to help in the struggle. It deals with both the children and their parents. Karim believes it is a phenomenal play.

Karim's next experience was touring all over the country with the play, *Joseph and the Amazing Technicolored Dream Coat*. Later, he toured with the play, *Blues in the Night*, a small blues musical review. After these productions, he felt it was time for him to "raise the bar" and set higher goals for himself.

Karim decided it was now time for him to return to Boston to be near his family. He was able to design shows for several productions at Mount Holyoke College. This opened doors for other work in the Boston area.

Following 9/11 in 2001, the theatre business took a big hit. Karim found it necessary to go back to being an electrician; but he also turned this situation into something good by taking classes to learn new technology. This opened doors for him to work in films and television.

His hard work and enthusiasm paved the way for even more opportunities. He was only 24 years old when he became the lighting director for the Boston Ballet. During the next five years he had other career experiences which included a trip around the world.

Karim enjoyed these challenges, but decided it was time to move to New York City to seek new opportunities. He was right! He became involved in films and television, including MSNBC. He also was able to continue another love, photography. He opened a photography shop. The highlight for him was meeting and marrying his wife, Gillian, who was working for a publishing company.

In 2011 Karim was offered a teaching position at his Alma Mater, West Virginia Wesleyan College. Being a professor had been one of his goals since he had been a college student. His wife, Gillian, encouraged him to fulfill this goal. She was willing to quit her job and finish her college education at Wesleyan. They had a good experience at Wesleyan. Karim not only taught theatre courses, but also did the design and technical work for Wesleyan's theatre productions.

After two years at Wesleyan he felt he needed to return to New York City. Karim believes he has had an amazing journey. He has traveled to every state in the USA except Hawaii and Alaska as well as spending time overseas. He has also been able to work in many facets of the theatre which he loves. Because of his hard work and creative abilities he has many rewards and successes.

Karim shares the following tips:

1. If you make up your mind to succeed, you will.
2. If you are willing to work, there is no such thing as believing something is impossible.
3. Use every tool at your disposal to succeed.
4. Don't give up.

JENNIFER BUZA

How would you feel sitting in the hall in elementary school because your teacher didn't want you in the classroom? She couldn't teach you and she told you it was because you were too dumb. Jennifer Buza needed to learn differently but she was not dumb. Today she is president and owner of the JB Logistic Company in Indianapolis, Indiana. She is an outstanding business woman.

Jen's Story

Jennifer grew up in a very supportive home with parents who encouraged her and helped her cope with her learning disabilities—dyslexia and Attention Deficit Disorder (ADD). Although her mother was a good advocate, attended all IEP (individual education plan) meetings, and pushed for better staffing at the school, Jen had some painful experiences in school which she has not forgotten. When she was in second grade, Jennifer's teacher did not know how to help her. She made Jennifer sit in the hall where she would not disturb anyone while reading or working on assignments. This was a lonely and frustrating experience for Jen. It occurred again in a high school Spanish class. There Jen was joined in the hall by two boys. The teacher did not think they could learn Spanish and she didn't want to hold back the rest of the class trying to teach them. In algebra class Jennifer's difficulties learning the material frustrated her resource teacher, a person hired by the state to teach learning disabled students. As a result of the teacher's problems in understanding how Jennifer learned, the frustrated teacher threw a book at her and told her she was stupid.

Despite these bad experiences Jen had other outstanding teachers who helped her cope. One of these good teachers whom she will always remember is Mrs. Traxell. She cared about the students and didn't expect everyone to learn the same way. Jennifer said she was ahead of her time. She praised Jen for her memorization ability, and helped her with phonics which was difficult for Jen. She understood that Jennifer was a good sight word reader, and did not penalize her for having problems with phonics. Jennifer achieved and enjoyed her class.

Jen's parents sent her to a private high school hoping she would have better experiences there. It was a good school, but she did not like being sent to a resource room, which was an off campus mobile unit furnished by the local school district. The students made fun of her and the other resource students. Today we would call this bullying! This made her feel different and contributed to feelings of inadequacy and low self-esteem. She will never forget these bad experiences, and they haunt her today. As a result, Jennifer still has feelings of inadequacy and is driven to be successful to prove people, especially teachers, wrong about her. However, despite Jennifer's feelings, friends and employees like her and consider her very successful.

College was a much better experience for Jen. She appreciated Wesleyan's Learning Center where she learned how to learn, and found advisors and teachers who were not only very helpful but also went "the second mile." She did, however, hate the Lindamood-Bell ® Program because she felt she was doing elementary phonics. In retrospect she knows it helped her. She enjoyed her public relations major and her professors. Jennifer worked hard in college, often feeling she had to work harder than her friends. Her hard work paid off as she graduated in four years; many LD students took an extra semester or two to graduate.

Jen has great organizing skills both personally and professionally. These have been helpful in accounting for her success since graduating from Wesleyan. She interned and then was hired to work for the San Jose Sharks farm team. She was with them for 2 years. She not only worked hard for the company, but also organized a community project, Carkner's Christmas, partnering with a defensive hockey player, Matt Carkner. This became an annual event and they worked with inner city schools providing gifts for children, such as mattresses, sheets, bikes, and other presents to meet their basic needs. They also provided the parents with grocery gift cards so that no one would go hungry.

After working 2 years with the Sharks, Jen took a position as National Marketing Manager for the Disney Company working in Elgin, Illinois. This was another good experience where she did well, but in two or three years she was ready for a change. She began working with a transportation company and successfully helped them to arrange transportation for other companies. Her superiors recognized her outstanding capabilities and greatly respected her. But the economy entered "The Great Recession" in 2008 and the company had to close.

As a creative and determined person, Jen turned this negative situation into a positive experience. She was inspired to take the leap of faith and begin her own company. She said she had people who wanted to work, and customers who liked her and appreciated her honesty and careful attention to detail. They were glad to give their business to her, rather than to some of the competitors. She is now owner and president of JB Logistics. Beginning in Elgin, Illinois, which is in the Chicago area, she moved her company to Indianapolis, Indiana, because she says it is, "The Heart of Transportation." Jen works with companies that need materials transported, and arranges for others to transport them. She enjoys her work and her staff. She likes to hire and help family-oriented people and is willing to teach employees, especially if they want to learn.

Jennifer not only finds her work rewarding, but also wants to be a part of the community in other ways. She volunteers with the Highland Group, whose purpose is to find grants for high school students. They have an outstanding program: "Steps for Success." As part of this program, they give a battery of seven tests to find student's strengths and gifts. As a result of the tests they are able to direct high school students into the appropriate field for pursuing their interests and talents. Jen is dedicated to helping these students. She teaches young people to "learn how to learn." Since she really enjoys teaching people who want to learn, she tries to help them realize that every one learns differently, and everyone has gifts. Therefore they can succeed!

Jennifer's tips for young people:

1. Find out how you learn.
2. Hard work pays off.
3. Find the right college.
4. Don't let anyone tell you that you can't do something.

JEFFREY KULINSKY

Jeffrey Kulinsky is a 2001 graduate of West Virginia Wesleyan College. A first grade teacher said he could never learn to read. Today he regularly reads legal briefs as a successful lawyer in the Chicago area.

Jeffrey "Jeff" Kulinsky's Story

Jeff was highly successful in college and law school, but he had some painful experiences in his earlier educational journey.

The first painful experience he remembers was in first grade (Jeff was around 6 or 7 years old) when he overheard his first grade teacher tell his mother, Lois Kulinsky, that he was dumb and would never amount to anything. Jeff remembers being so upset that he just wanted to cry. His mother did not believe the teacher, and she made an appointment to have Jeff tested at the Searle Learning Clinic at Northwestern University where he was diagnosed with a learning disability, dyslexia. Diagnostic test results indicated that he had an above average IQ and adult reasoning skills. As a result of the diagnosis, Jeff was put into special education classes, occupational therapy, and Jeff's mother arranged for him to receive help from a reading and spelling tutor.

During this period Lois's father was helpful and encouraging to her, telling her that Jeff would be fine. They were words she needed to hear and helped her as she became his advocate and special support person. Her father was also helpful to Jeff. He was a wonderful grandfather and they had a great relationship. Jeff remembers him saying, "Jeff, if you really want something, work for it and you will succeed." This was good advice which Jeff believed then and believes now. They are words to live by.

A little later when Jeff was around 7 years old his mother took him to see Dr. Harold Levinson, an MD in New York who was a Clinical Associate Professor of Psychiatry at the New York Medical Center and director and founder of the Medical Dyslexic Treatment Center in Great Neck, New York. Dr. Levinson ran a number of tests on Jeff to determine what, if anything, he might be able to do to help treat Jeff's dyslexia.

After extensive testing, Dr. Levinson recommended a number of health food products and a few medications that, when used together, helped change Jeff's life. Within hours of being on the medications the world seemed clearer and Jeff went from not being able to walk in a straight line or focus for long periods of time to being able to do both. Jeff's mother noticed these changes immediately even if Jeff did not.

The medicine was also helpful for him in overcoming fears. He had been dominated by fears of doing numerous things. He had been afraid to go on a high carnival ride. He didn't ride escalators in the stores because he saw the stairs as different waves. Now he could ride them. He became much more secure and was able to tackle other obstacles he had feared such as social issues and reading.

Dr. Levinson recommended that he receive recorded books for the blind. Jeff had found reading frustrating at an early age due to being unable to focus and not being able to decode (sound out the words); yet as a young child, he loved being read to and listening to stories. Jeff began listening to recorded books every night before he would go to sleep. Listening to these books was the start of Jeff's lifelong love of reading.

When Jeff was nine years old a breakthrough in his reading occurred when he received the Lindamood-Bell ® reading program. It was through the tutor's use of this program that Jeff learned to read and it enabled him to become the avid reader he is today.

Jeff's mother continued to take him to see Dr. Levinson in New York once a year, until Jeff was 21 years old. During these trips she took Jeff to see three to five Broadway Musicals a year. Jeff loves theater to this day.

Jeff continued to progress from a combination of schooling, tutors, and medication throughout grammar school. At the time Jeff made the transition to middle school, reading, math, and social skills were Jeff's biggest weaknesses.

Jeff's first year in junior high school was one of the most trying times in his life, both educationally and socially. During elementary school all the children in special education within the local school districts were kept together in special education classes at one school. Upon entering junior high school, all of those children including Jeff were split up and sent back to their home districts. On top of the move to a new school, Jeff was assigned to a special education teacher who was not trained to teach children with learning disabilities. The lack of a skilled teacher, combined with a new foreign social environment and not knowing anyone at the new school created an environment where Jeff was unable to succeed academically or socially.

The longer Jeff stayed at the school, the more he felt cut off and isolated from his peers. He was bullied, made fun of, and beaten up at recess a number of times. It got to the point where the thought of even going to school would give Jeff stomach pains. He found a coping strategy and for the first time in his life started to pick up and read books on his own. Although his reading was slow at the time (getting through 10 pages could take him an hour), he kept reading. The books were his refuge from a world in which he felt he just didn't fit in.

Jeff's mother was pleased he had found a coping strategy, but she was a "determined advocate," and decided to tackle the school system. As a lawyer she had knowledge of effective strategies for change. She hired an attorney who specialized in special education issues. He accompanied her to the school. She was particularly concerned about Jeff's IEP (Individual Educational Plan). Mrs. Kulinski also informed the school he needed recorded textbooks and showed them procedures for getting them. As a result, the school hired Jeff's tutor to tutor his teachers in ways to help him and others.

Jeff's mother, seeing he was still having a bad experience in the junior high school, transferred him to a private school, Cove School, in Glencoe, Illinois. In this school 99% of the students were learning disabled. He liked Cove school and was liked by teachers and students. Jeff spent the rest of junior high school and high school at Cove School. Because of his teachers there, he regained his writing and reading abilities, plus the confidence he had lost from his first year of junior high. (When Jeff graduated from college, he was asked to return to Cove School and to speak to their graduates.)

Jeff loved to travel. The family went to Europe, the Caribbean, Florida, and the Grand Canyon and on an Alaskan Cruise. When he was on a cruise at age 13, he didn't want to join the activities for teenagers. His mother insisted. He loved it so much after being forced to go to one activity that throughout the rest of the cruise he would be with the other teenagers all day. His mother only saw him at breakfast and dinner.

During Jeff's last two years of high school at Cove, he took selected mainstream classes at Glenbrook South High School. Lois was pleased her son had this opportunity, but had fears about the school system because of her previous experience with the public school. She asked for a meeting with school officials, and probably went with a chip on her shoulder. She was very surprised and pleased at their willingness to provide all the services required on his IEP and to pay for these expenses, unlike his junior high school.

When Jeff was a high school junior, he participated in a college fair. I was one of several college professors attending, and after interviewing him encouraged him to visit Wesleyan. With prodding from his mother he took a chance and attended the Wesleyan Learning Center's summer program before his last year of high school. After having a great time in the summer program, receiving an A in the college level psychology course that was part of it, and being offered a scholarship, he decided to attend Wesleyan.

At Wesleyan, Jeff's confidence in himself grew as his successes grew and he knew he would be successful. He really liked his advisor, Lynn Neaves. He knew she cared about him and would help him in all areas of his life. Lynn says she was impressed with him, especially his work ethic and his determination. He took advantage of the services of the

Learning Center which he felt helped him academically. He appreciated his professors, the Learning Center and the opportunity he had to work as a student assistant in the Learning Center computer lab. Since he was a computer information science major, his service was valued there. At Wesleyan, not only did he succeed academically, but also grew socially. He became involved with the international student organization through his roommate, who was from India, and made a lot of new friends as well as learning about many different cultures. He still keeps in touch with these friends today.

After graduating from Wesleyan, Jeff returned to Illinois, but was not able to find a computer position. For a little over a year, he worked three jobs: retail, tech support, and substitute teaching, while looking for a computer programming position. He eventually moved to Florida where he worked as a computer programmer at System Data Resource, writing software for PDA's and cell phones. After a year of programming, Jeff decided he did not want to program for the rest of his life and resigned his programming position. He took a job doing tech support at Office2Go and used his extra time to study for the LSAT.

Jeff took the LSAT only once and got an acceptable score. It was not the best score but he did not let that discourage him. He applied to multiple law schools and got accepted to a Florida law school, the John Marshal law school summer program, and also Thomas M. Cooley Law School in Michigan. Jeff decided to go to Thomas M. Cooley because they offered him a 40% scholarship. There he used his hard earned study skills, and the work ethic engrained into him from his mother and grandfather, tutors, Cove School teachers, and the Wesleyan Learning Center staff. He earned straight A's his first year at law school.

During law school Jeff interned with Judge Jeffrey Lawrence as his law clerk, worked for the Illinois States Attorney as a 711 student lawyer, and interned with the law firm of Rinella and Rinella. Jeff graduated from law school magna cum laude and 12th in his class!

After studying and passing the bar on his first try in July 2008, Jeff began working at his mother's law firm, Lois Kulinsky & Associates, Ltd., doing family law, probate, estate planning, and corporate law. Jeff works hard, but loves his work. He knows he has found the right career to use his gifts and talents.

Jeff's Tips

1. Don't let fear control your actions.
2. When developing your reading skills, read what interests you.
3. Persevere! When you are fearful that you can't do something, make it your goal to do it.
4. If you really want something, work for it, and you will succeed. (His Grandfather Ben's advice)

NICK SELAN

Nick is unusual. Most people like to do things that are easy for them so they can do well—such as easier college majors or future careers. But not Nick! Nick chose subjects that were hard for him because he wanted to learn, to do well, and prove that he could succeed. Science and math were hard for Nick because of his learning disability. Therefore he majored in physics. Nick is a 2004 graduate of West Virginia Wesleyan. His wife, Theresa, is also a Wesleyan graduate. Nick is currently a teacher and chairman of the science department at Moravian Academy in Bethlehem, Pennsylvania.

Nick's Story

Nick does not remember the first few years of elementary school as a happy time. His first grade teacher believed he was lazy. His second grade teacher suspected a learning disability but he was not tested. His third grade teacher originally thought he was lazy but by the end of the school year she began to believe Nick had some type of learning problem.

Shortly before school began in the fall of his fourth grade year, Nick asked his mother if she could arrange for him to be in Mrs. Devaney's fourth grade class. When his mother asked why, he told her that Mrs. Devaney challenged the students and asked question before they went out for recess. He wanted to be able to answer those questions. His mother was pleased with his answer and the administration seemed to be too because he was placed in her fourth grade room. This proved to be a good decision as it was Mrs. Devaney who realized that Nick had more ability than he was showing. She recommended he be tested for the gifted program. Her intuition was correct. Nick was gifted! However, he was not only gifted, but also had a learning disability. The results of his tests indicated that he had Attention Deficit Disorder, and had learning problems in reading and writing.

Discovering he was gifted was the beginning of a much happier period for Nick as he joined the gifted class each week and finally felt academically challenged. He continued to do the course work that he originally felt was too easy so he would be allowed to attend the gifted classes.

Nick remembers math being difficult. His difficulty was one some other gifted students have had. In a workshop on the gifted that I attended many years ago, I heard Dr. Walter Barbe, then editor of *Highlights Magazine,* tell the story about a young man who was gifted, but failing math. This young man was on the *Quiz Kids* radio program, amazing listeners with his ability to answer difficult math problems by doing them in his head. Dr. Barbe said unfortunately this student was failing 6th grade math because he could not write out his methods for solving the problems. Nick had this same problem. His teachers wanted to see how he got the answers. He did not know. His mother told me he said, "There aren't any methods; there is just the answer." He remembers being embarrassed in an algebra class because the teacher said he was cheating since he couldn't write down how he got the answers. This was painful and upsetting for Nick. However he was encouraged when he heard **an** interview with Nobel Prize winner, Dr. Richard Feynman, who also did the algebra problems in his head and had difficulties similar to Nick's. Nick describes an experience when he was told he was doing algebra "wrong." He took great offense at this because he was getting the right answers by doing it his way; obviously it was not "wrong." Nick describes algebra not as a series of steps in all cases, but in a sort of graphical or special way that is difficult to write down.

Nick remembers three other problems with math. He had great difficulty memorizing the multiplication tables in elementary school and remembers not being able to go out for recess, but having to stay with the teacher to try to master them. He had similar problems learning long division. In college he was forced to drop pre-calculus, because he was failing it. This was painful for him as he had never failed a class, and had passed pre-calculus in high school. His high school teacher had advised the students to take it as a review. He was able to go on to calculus 1, but again met failure making a D and later dropped calculus 2 when he was failing it. Nick was determined not to allow these failures to prevent him from majoring in physics. In the summer after his sophomore year, he enrolled at Ohio University. He was determined to succeed and he did, passing both calculus 1 and 2!

Buckhannon, West Virginia as well as West Virginia Wesleyan were known to Nick before he entered college. His grandparents, Lillian and Jim Halverson lived in Buckhannon and his Selan Grandparents, Iris and John, lived in a nearby town. In a sense, Wesleyan was a safe place.

His grandmother, Dr. Lillian Halverson, was a professor at Wesleyan. She was familiar with the Learning Center's Summer Institute Program. Since Dr. Halverson had taught some students who had participated in the program, she felt attending the summer institute would be a good opportunity for Nick and encouraged his parents to send him. Dr. Halverson was right: The summer institute was a good experience for him. He said for the first time in his life, he felt on a "level playing field" with his peers. He realized he was not inferior to the others. This attitude boosted his confidence which actually was one of the goals of the program. He did very well. The program was designed for students to take a non-credit study skills course and a regular credit freshman psychology course. The psychology course was taught by Dr. Richard Calef, a popular Wesleyan psychology professor. Dr. Calef had the ability to make psychology "come alive", and to relate to the students in a positive way. Nick recalls the institute as a wonderful academic experience with additional fun filled activities! Each summer at the close of the program a scholarship to Wesleyan was given to the outstanding student. Nick received it. He reflected that the scholarship was a great boost to his confidence by assuring him he could do well in his studies during his senior year in high school, and by realizing he would be ready for college.

Nick said he loved the summer program and decided he wanted to teach in a similar program in the future. He fulfilled this dream! Ever since graduating from college he has participated each summer in academic camps or programs. He taught astronomy four summers at Gettysburg College in Pennsylvania; taught forensic science one summer at Heidelberg College in Ohio; and has been at Centenary College in New Jersey for four summers. At Centenary he has taught forensic science, and currently is the director of their summer program. Through these experiences, Nick believes he is helping others as he was helped.

After Nick's summer experience at Wesleyan, his senior year in high school seemed to go fast. The scholarship to Wesleyan and the summer institute made Wesleyan his number 1 choice for college. Since Nick likes challenges he decided to major in physics. He said he not only was interested in the subject, but also wanted to prove to himself and others he could major in it and succeed. He did! Nick especially appreciated two physics professors, Dr. Joe Wiest and Dr. Burt Popson.

Dr. Wiest recognized Nick's ability and was always encouraging and motivating him to do his best. Nick said that Dr Wiest understood problems of students with ADD, and often in a kind way kept Nick on task and focused. Although the physics courses were not easy, Nick found them challenging and very interesting. He studied and worked hard.

One of Nick's best experiences in college was playing in the jazz band. In fifth grade he began playing in the band and enjoyed it throughout middle and senior high school. He not only was in the band, but also played viola in the orchestra from fourth grade through middle school. Music is a wonderful outlet. Co-curricular activities are important!

When Nick graduated from Wesleyan in 2004, he felt he needed time off from classes to decide on his future career. During the next year and a half, he did substitute teaching and graduate work at Marshall University in Huntington, West Virginia. After a semester at Marshall, Nick began a masters' degree at Miami University of Ohio. He had done well at Marshall, but they did not have the program he wanted. Miami

University was a good experience and he received a Master's in Physics with a concentration in planetary astrophysics.

After receiving his Master's Degree, Nick realized teaching was to be his future career. Following graduation he had an opportunity to teach at his Alma Mater, West Virginia Wesleyan. Dr. Wiest had followed Nick's career. As a result, he recommended Nick for a position as an instructor in the physics department at Wesleyan for the spring semester in 2009. This was a great challenge for Nick. He taught a Geology Course and the Geology lab. In addition he directed other labs in the department and advised and assisted a senior with her research at Green Bank Radio Astronomy Observatory. In May Term, he taught an astronomy course and directed the astronomy lab. At the end of May term he taught forensics during the summer camp at Centenary College. Teaching on the college level was challenging and Nick hopes someday he might earn a PhD and become a college professor.

In the fall of 2009 he began teaching at Blessed Trinity Catholic High School in Roswell, Georgia, where he taught for four years. In the fall of 2013 he began a new challenge, becoming a teacher and Chairperson of the Science Department at Moravian Academy, a preparatory school founded in 1742 in Bethlehem, Pa.

Family is important to Nick. When I asked him to share his most painful experience, it was not about his disability or educational experiences; instead it dealt with family. After college and during the period of graduate school, three of Nick's grandparents died, Jim Halverson and Iris and John Selan. He loved them very much. They were always there for him at happy and sad times. It was hard to think of living without them. He was glad they had all known his wife, Theresa, but sorry that his children would not know them.

In addition to being a good student, teacher, and administrator, Nick is a good husband and father. He met his wife, Theresa, at the Learning Center at Wesleyan. They both were student assistants, supervising the computer lab. Nick and Theresa were married in December 2006 after both had graduated from college and pursued graduate studies. Their daughter, Imogen, was born in 2012. Before Imogen's birth, Theresa, who is a talented woman, had worked several years. She was the outreach educator at the Clay Center, a museum and performing arts center in

Charleston, West Virginia, and has been a substitute teacher. Presently she is enjoying being a full time mother. They are a wonderful caring family.

Nick has given the following tips:

1. Develop Time Management skills.
2. Plan time for homework and fun.
3. Get work done before play.
4. Develop confidence and believe in yourself.
5. It is okay to fail, but try again: Failing a class is not the end of the world.

Summer institute and special support students enjoyed bocce ball at Coston's home.

TIPS FOR PARENTS

This chapter's ideas are from a number of mothers; most, but not all of their children attended college. Their children are successful today. Many are included in *Celebration of Success*. The mothers are home makers, a teacher who is also dyslexic, business women, and lawyers. Obviously both parents need to be involved in helping their child but typically the mothers take the lead in dealing with the child's homework, teachers, and problems. These women have one thing in common. They are all parents of a Learning Disabled child or children. There are also stories shared by the students about their parents, and a sister shared about her sibling.

A dyslexic mother of four LD children said, "As a parent remember the child's LD is NOT your fault. Don't feel guilty! Talk to your child about the disability, letting him realize it is not his fault either. Assure him that he can learn coping strategies." Every mother with whom I spoke recommended learning all you can about the disability. Have the child tested. This often means a private source not the school system. Study! Understand the scores and what they mean. Share as much as you can with your child. Some parents have used the term "learning difference." One mother compared the need for glasses to the special needs of her learning disabled daughter. This worked, and helped her daughter feel better about herself. Her daughter is now a teacher and has used this strategy to help others.

Another common thread; all parents said, "Be your child's advocate." One mother stated, "Don't assume that the school officials know more than you do. That is not true. The only person your child can count on is **you**! No matter how rough it may get, no one cares about your child like you do." One young man told his mother and dad that once he knew they were behind him, he could accept his disability and move forward. Being an advocate doesn't always mean a confrontational advocate. There are some school systems that cooperate with parents and appreciate the parents' input. On the whole most schools today are more aware of learning disabilities than previously. However, they can be more effective if parents share with them. Several of my former students became LD teachers so they could help students and teachers.

There are no pat answers because every child and every parent handles the learning disability and the situation differently. Some parents found a private boarding school or a private school near relatives was best for the child even though it meant being away from home. Others have found tutors, special classes, and monitoring the child's progress in school worked for them. One mother worked with the school system closely, helping in the classroom not only with her own son but also with others. She found cooperating with the school worked for her and her son. Other parents have had to become assertive advocates even suing the school system. Attending IEP (Individual Educational Plan) meetings and making sure the IEP is being carried out is important. If cooperation isn't possible, one mother reminded me that there are organizations that will provide legal aid free or for a low fee. The major goal is allowing the children to succeed, accept themselves, and understand their abilities as well as their disabilities.

The students I interviewed talked about how much they appreciated their parents. They knew their parents gave up their own time together or time to participate in groups, etc. to help with the child's homework. For some parents and students, working together on homework assignments were good experiences; for others they were disasters. At those disastrous times it is necessary to realize the child's frustrations and also help the child realize you have bad days too. Don't hesitate in saying, "I am sorry." For those who found helping with homework an unpleasant situation, hiring someone such as a retired teacher was exactly what was needed. For many, summer time experiences were good. One mother had to drive a long way to the private summer school, but she and her son enjoyed their time together in the car, and her son appreciated being rewarded with a treat each day. For some, working together and then having play or swimming time was great. For others going to Mac Donald's was the right approach. One mother said she always allowed her son to pay the bill, and he developed math skills which resulted in math becoming his favorite subject and one where he excelled. Family trips were pleasant ways to enrich their educational experiences. These often helped with history or geography. "Different Strokes for Different Folks" is a good phrase to remember.

Many parents have shared with me that having an LD child in the family often becomes a family affair. One of my friends shared the following story. She remembers that her brother had a tough time reading and their mother would sit with him at the kitchen table for hours helping him. She said now she knows her brother probably had dyslexia, but in the 1960's help wasn't often available. She shared the following story about her brother: "He would hold his hand over the first letter of the word "was" or "saw" so that he could identify the first letter in order to read the word. He was so excited when they started having audio books. He told me once that he never wanted to read a book that didn't have pictures. I asked him why and he said, 'the pictures help me know what the book is about because sometimes I just can't read the words.' I was shocked! My younger brother and I had no problem reading, but we were so jealous of him because he was a phenomenal artist, and we couldn't draw a straight line with a ruler. I told him that once and he said, 'At least you can read!' After that I helped him by reading parts of the books to him when he had book reports and other assignments."

I have heard similar stories many times. Former First Lady Barbara Bush shared at a Learning Disability conference. She said that one of her sons who was in second grade was home from school with a cold. She read to him, and then wanted him to read to her. She discovered he could not read! Since he was a very intelligent boy he had been able to fool his first grade teacher because the pictures gave him clues for reading the words. Barbara was not only able to help her son, but also she was able to work with the school enabling him to get the help he needed.

The importance of families working together helps the child not only succeed with school work, but also shows him they care. These are important ways to build self-esteem which is vital for success. Almost all the parents interviewed felt it was important for the child to discover his abilities, talents, and interests. For many this was sports, for others music, art, or drama. There are a variety of interests and activities, but the important thing is that everyone needs to find enjoyment and success. This is wonderful for building self-confidence. Many of the students about whom I have written receive college scholarships based on their achievements in their special interests.

The problem of bullying is being more actively addressed today. LD children are often more vulnerable and become the targets. Frequently they don't handle the situations well, causing them to become the one in trouble. One mother said she told her son that if a child started fighting not to strike back, but to fall down. This saved him from being the one punished. It also prevented his peers from making fun of him for being a coward. Helping the child develop strategies to cope with difficult situations is important.

Mrs. Joyce Leo, mother of Diane Leo Menorca, has summarized the above tips in this chapter and added others of her own. Here is her composite of tips which I believe will be a helpful reference for many parents today:

1. Don't feel guilty.
2. Explain to the child that everyone has strengths and weaknesses. Learn about the Disabilities Act and how it affects your child. Learn about coping strategies and help your child develop them.
3. Take advantage of all technological support, such as audio books, speech writing, educational videos, etc.
4. Take children to all learning environments—museums, history centers, touring factories where things are made such as Hershey's Chocolate Factory, etc., in addition to all family fun places of entertainment.
5. Educate yourself about dyslexia and learning differences.

6. Have your child tested by competent, language/neurological specialists as early as "great difficulties" are reported in school.
7. Find something every day that your child is good at; praise that. Do everything possible to support a child's self-esteem which is often shattered when they can't keep up in reading, writing, and spelling at school.
8. Focus on developing a working vocabulary so the child can express himself or herself verbally. Dyslexics are often gifted at speaking. (examples: John F. Kennedy, Robert Kennedy, Edward Kennedy, who were all tutored in early childhood with multi-sensory education; George W. Bush and Nelson Rockefeller, who had assistants read for them and take their verbal dictation for speeches—all excelled in politics.)
9. Work with a positive attitude with the public school system. It may or may not be able to provide the appropriate education. If it is possible, volunteer to help and make yourself as parent a welcome sight; if not, and if you are able, hire a tutor, or retired teacher to give individual attention. If all else fails, and you are able, place your child in a boarding school specializing in learning differences. The cost is well worth it when the child graduates and is prepared to take his or her proper role in society.
10. Above all, be patient, supportive, and loving. And don't forget that if you have other children who are not dyslexic they need their own special attention too. Oftentimes, the family is so overwhelmed with the one child having difficulty, they will try to move heaven and earth to help that child, and the other children may feel "left out" if they are not included in the picture and then given their own space to shine in their own way.
11. Above all, remember that it is a stressful experience on all the family to diagnose and treat the dyslexic child. Try to make the entire process a challenge to overcome with unity and positivism. Many marriages can flounder; sibling rivalry may emerge; and the LD child may sink in spirits, even blaming themselves for all the upheaval that can arise.

12. Above all, teach them resilience and inner strength to withstand the often painful misunderstandings they will encounter in their lives. And let them know they are perfectly okay the way they are. God made them that way.

TIPS FOR TEACHERS

Many people have asked what methods or techniques did you and your staff use that resulted in such good success. Upon reflecting on this question, I know it is impossible to give a specific answer. Since everyone learns differently, methods vary with each student. My first priority is to accept students where they are and then seek to know each student's interests, needs, and abilities. This requires some informal time with the students where the student does the majority of talking and the teacher listens with interest. In this way you get to know the person, and the person knows that you care. Teachers' and students' attitudes are keys for success.

There are some methods that are important for everyone and can be done in group situations. Building students' self-esteem, inspiring their determination, and teaching techniques for achieving academic success are all necessary and are inseparable.

One of the most important ways for teachers to help students succeed is to build their self-esteem. It is often more appropriate for some students to have shorter assignments. They can learn as much by doing eight math problems well as by doing ten or twelve, and this allows a student to keep up with the class and have a feeling of success. Individualization can have amazing results. The child is more important than the content. We are all unique and a method that works for one student may not work for another. It is vital to good teaching to avoid criticizing and "putting people down", especially in front of the whole class. This is true for all students. It has been said that it takes seven positive statements to counteract one negative statement. A wise principal told his staff, "You get more flies with honey than you do with vinegar." I practiced this and I tried to remember Mr. Rogers's statement as he began his TV shows, "You are special."

A student needs determination to accompany self-esteem. While some are already highly motivated, others need to have ways provided to help them develop determination and perseverance. After getting a bad grade, students need an advisor, teacher, or counselor to help them set realistic goals and to offer help on how to do better next time. One of the most frequent tips offered by the successful persons in this book is the advice to never give up. Sometimes this means going for what seems to others an impossible dream.

Teaching good study methods to use when doing homework or class work is vital for a student in learning how to succeed. Students need to know, "It is not the hours you put in, but what you put in the hours" that makes a difference. All students should be taught this, but it is especially needed for LD students who often have problems studying, because of poor study methods and slow work habits. For some students, tutors or classroom aids should be used in such a way that the LD student does not feel "different." Following the guide lines of the Americans With Disabilities Act is vital. One of the most important accommodations for many is being allowed to take exams un-timed and in a special environment where they feel comfortable.

Most LD students have problems in reading. When I taught reading, I was constantly reminded that each person learns in their own way. Many dyslexics see words differently, which makes them slow readers and adds to their frustration. It is important to teach all students, especially slow readers, to develop the skill of seeing an "eyeful" of words. Reading each individual word is not only slow but also can hurt one's comprehension. Brain research has taught us that the short term memory can only hold seven items. When we have sentences with more than seven words, we may forget the first words before finishing the sentence, and this hurts our understanding of the entire sentence. It will take practice to develop this skill. Previewing a chapter of nonfiction material is another important skill to teach. "We get out of the printed page what we bring to it." Many teachers have known this for years, and now brain research has verified it. Comprehension can improve as much as eighty percent with previewing. Many students fight against doing this and say it takes too much time, but actually it saves time. I have had students who finally realized this and have asked, "Why wasn't I taught this in elementary or high school?"

A comprehension technique used by some study skills and reading teachers, and by those teaching the Lindamood-Bell ® reading program, is a method known as "visualizing verbalizing." This has been developed by Nanci Bell, co-founder of the Lindamood-Bell ® reading program. In this program students are taught: first, visualize a picture and then verbalize it. Secondly, visualize a word and then verbalize it. Thirdly, visualize a sentence and verbalize it. Fourthly, visualize a whole paragraph and verbalize it. This is a powerful method to improve comprehension! As students practice this process, they become more proficient in their ability to put into words exactly what they want to say. This transfers into better writing skills as well.

Many of the people in *Celebration of Success* are teachers. I believe their disability has helped them become effective teachers. I am concluding this chapter with philosophy and tips by Jonathan Langsam, Patricia Boothe, Amy Shearman O'Brien, and Emily Hogan.

Jonathan Langsam suggests teachers and parents look up the Circle of Courage Website. This approach has merit in the class room and is worth trying. It has four components. The first is the spirit of belonging. The Native American culture has an emphasis on belonging to the community. This sense of belonging can be encouraged in the classroom. The second is the spirit of mastery which focuses on four levels: physical, cognitive, social, and spiritual. As has been stated earlier, it is important for a student to feel successful. The Native Americans also recommend the importance of seeing others achieve and praising them. Third is the spirit of independence. It is sometimes difficult for teachers and parents to find the balance between pushing a child into independence too soon, or holding him back when he is ready to achieve on his own. The fourth component is generosity. Children need to learn at an early age about giving to others. It helps them realize that people are more important than things.

Jonathan also recommends teachers look at reclaimingyouth.com. which is also a part of "Circle of Courage." This section emphasizes that if one of the four elements in the circle is not met, disappointment occurs which can result in unhealthy behavior. As stated in his story, Jonathan believes it is important for teachers to try to understand the pain learning disabled and emotionally disturbed students experience, as well as the effects of punishment and coercion. Helping students accept ownership and responsibility for their actions is vital.

Jonathan urges teachers to be creative. Although he knows that teachers are under pressure to cover so much material and are tied to their curriculum, he urges them to slow down and not worry about the pressures. It is especially true with LD students, that teachers accept and teach them where they are. He uses the alphabet as an example. He tells teachers not to worry about getting from A to Z, but meet them at C and prepare them for D, E, and F next year. "Just because a kid can't learn 2+2 in six months, doesn't mean he is not going to be ready for it with the next teacher. The most important thing is that the child sitting in front of you has a positive experience. Teach the child not the subject. I believe this is good advice for most students, and accounts for the success of most of my former students who are in *Celebration of Success*...

In the article about Patricia Boothe in *The Salem Times Register* and in her story in this book, her philosophy of teaching is illustrated with tips. She believes children need to know what is expected of them, and teachers need to remember to meet individual needs of students in a caring way. Be flexible and give positive reinforcement. These are similar to tips already given, but illustrate their importance.

Amy Shearman O'Brien is not only a successful teacher but the mother of four LD children. In addition to suggesting many of the tips which have been mentioned, Amy emphasized the importance of teachers who may have some type of handicap or problem sharing their struggles and failures. Teachers need to help LD students recognize their gifts and understand that everyone learns differently. She suggests a class do research on famous LD persons, recognizing the struggles these people had. Amy recommends that as homework, LD students make flash cards and review class notes at night. (I agree. I always told students, "Review your notes daily because you forget more in the first 8 hours than you do the next six months.") Amy shares the wisdom of her parents with her classes. Her mother told her, "At times you may have to take two steps backward to make two steps forward. Even if you fail, as long as you know in your heart you did your best that is all that matters." As a teacher, Amy believed she needed to know why students were not succeeding and what makes them tick. She recommends, "Be sensitive to the student with a behavior problem; often it is a cover up for not admitting having an LD."

Emily Hogan agrees with the others about the importance of self-confidence. She says, "I find that self-confidence is a huge obstacle for students—both with learning differences and without. Every student can learn; but I think teachers need to find the way that each child learns most effectively. It does take going above and beyond the normal expectation of a teacher at times. Sometimes this might even involve adjusting assessments and the way you grade students. I also think it is incredibly important to have a strong relationship with parents of all of the children in your class. You each need an honest and supportive relationship."

IN MEMORIAM

During the period in which this book was being written, four classmates of these successful people in *Celebration of Success* died. Three of them had been interviewed to be part of the book. We give thanks for their lives.

Jim Bemis, 1997 Wesleyan graduate
Bill Brady, 1990 Wesleyan graduate
Shannon Stirrup Pitney, 1993 Wesleyan graduate
Michael Tate, 1990 Wesleyan graduate

Edwards Brothers Malloy
Oxnard, CA USA
August 21, 2013